OUTWARD JOURNEY

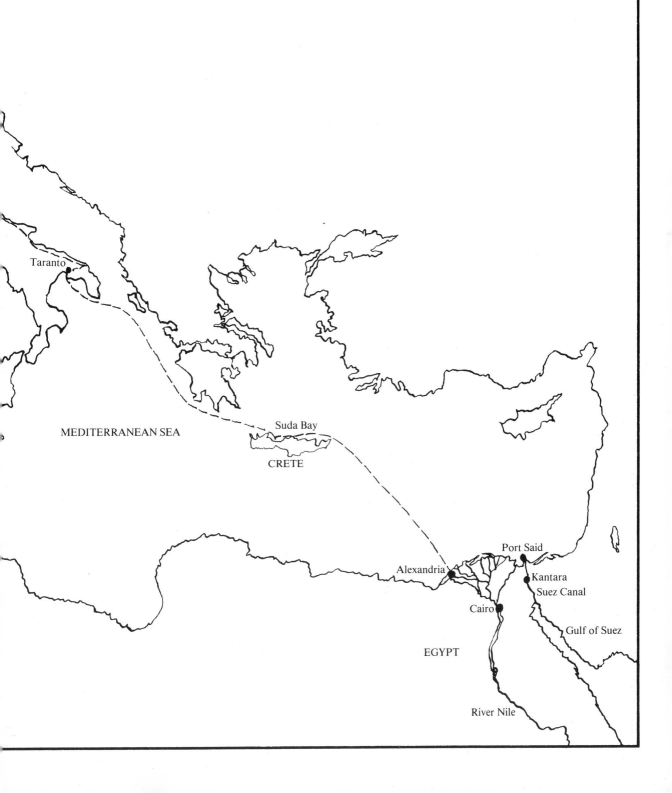

Taranto

MEDITERRANEAN SEA

Suda Bay

CRETE

Port Said

Alexandria

Kantara
Suez Canal

Cairo

Gulf of Suez

EGYPT

River Nile

GREAT UNCLE FRED'S WAR

AN ILLUSTRATED DIARY

1917 – 1920

GREAT UNCLE FRED'S WAR

AN ILLUSTRATED DIARY

1917–1920

Researched and Edited

by

Alan Pryor and Jenifer K. Woods

PRYOR PUBLICATIONS

©PRYOR PUBLICATIONS 1985
75 Dargate Road, Yorkletts,
Whitstable, Kent CT5 3AE
England

British Library Cataloguing in Publication Data.

Mills, Fred
    Great uncle Fred's war: an illustrated diary
    1917 – 1920
    1. Great Britain. *Army* 2. World War, 1914 – 1918
    – Campaigns – Turkey and the Near East –
    Palestine
    I. Title II. Pryor, Alan III. Woods, Jenifer K.
    940.4'15'0924   D568.7

ISBN 0 946014 04 3

Researched and Edited by
Alan Pryor and Jenifer K. Woods

Cover Design by Alan Pryor

Artwork by David Shersby

Typesetting by
PGH Typesetting Ltd,
6 Granada House, Gabriels Hill,
Maidstone
Set in 11/12pt English Times
Justified to 35 pica ems

Photographic Reproductions by
Clan Studios, Bromley, Kent

Printed in Great Britain by
Oaten Hill Press, 35 Oaten Hill,
Canterbury, Kent

Bound by
Bookbinders of London Ltd.,
11 Ronalds Road, Highbury,
London N5 1XJ England

FOREWORD

Uncle Fred's Diary is remarkable for a number of reasons. In the first place, by military regulations it ought not to exist for soldiers during the first world war were forbidden to keep diaries. For that reason relatively few first-hand and immediate impressions by ordinary soldiers have survived. This is not to say, of course, that reminiscences of the first world war are rare, but most of them are from the pens of the privileged, educated, officer ranks. In fact most of them, certainly the most famous, are the work of men who, if they survived, became professional writers – the obvious examples are Graves, Sassoon, Blunden and Erich Maria Remarque; of those who did not survive the most enduring and powerful testaments are to be found in the searing poetry of Wilfred Owen, Isaac Rosenberg, Julian Grenfell and others of that tragic lost generation.

Yet Uncle Fred was no poet, he was not a man of letters, nor yet a philosopher. And in this we see another of the unusual aspects of this publication. It is the very absence of literary artifice which makes the diary so fresh and so immediate. Uncle Fred was not writing for an audience, nor with the critics in mind; he was recording in simple, effective, and transparently clear language what was going on around him in the bizarre and often absurd world into which the high politics of the European powers had plunged him and many millions of others. In that he served in Egypt and the Near East rather than on the western front his remarks and observations are of greater value for they concern a part of the war which is little commentated upon and often ignored.

So what does *Uncle Fred's Diary* tell us? It does not, of course, reveal anything "new" in the sense of unknown treaties, battles, secret agreements or events of that nature. Nevertheless, it is interesting to note, for example, that a number of naval vessels performing escort duty in the Mediterranean were Japanese; it is often forgotten that Japan had been Britain's ally longer than had France, and the Japanese contribution to the fighting in Europe is a neglected subject.

But the diary will not be read for what it reveals of high politics. It is a small piece of social history, and good social history at that. Reading through this diary one easily senses the feeling of somewhat bemuzed resentment at the behaviour and the attitude of the officers, and one traces the development of this puzzlement into an anger which is made the stronger by its restraint. The writer does not preach revolutionary doctrine or demand the total restructuring of the world, military or civilian; he simply asks why it is that there is such lack of consideration, such needless indifference to the needs of the thousands of ordinary soldiers. Finally, following from this point, the closing stages of the diary reveal a state of unrest amongst British troops which is perhaps not surprising and is certainly not unknown; on the other hand in Uncle Fred's experience it is also clear that after the armistice the officers in his small part of the war machine were amazingly unsure of their position and authority. The portrayal of the relations between officers and men immediately after the ending of hostilities is probably the most important feature, from the historian's point of view, of the whole diary.

Despite his frustrations Uncle Fred seems in later years to have looked back upon his war service with some nostalgia, and he willingly made his contribution to the second world war. He was certainly unaware that yet more decades later he would be making a posthumous contribution to our knowledge of the past. We can only hope that he would have gained as much satisfaction from seeing his diary published as we can from reading it.

R. J. CRAMPTON, Senior Lecturer in History, The University of Kent at Canterbury

CONTENTS

PREFACE

These diaries were discovered in a box of old photographs following my great-uncle's death in 1978. There were three sets of small loose-leaf pages, two of which were bound together with twists of rusty wire through the holes. All three had been written in pencil and placed inside a black leatherette cover. There was very little punctuation and I hope that I have interpreted them in the way he intended. His medals were with the diaries.

He was a lovely old man and as a child I looked forward to his visits because I knew that a crisp £1 note would be put in my hand before he left, but in the meantime I confess that I became very bored every time he said "Now I remember . . . ". How I wish that I had known then what questions to ask him; the preparation of this book would have been far easier had we been able to turn to him for the answers! He was just an ordinary soldier and a very small cog in the Great War, but to us he was always "Great Uncle Fred".

For several years I cherished the dream of seeing the diaries published and I would like to thank everyone who has helped and encouraged me:

— My immediate family for their individual help and support.

— The older members of the family who reminisced and answered endless questions, and who loaned me many of the photographs.

— Nina, who cared for Uncle for so many years and who recalls him reading the diaries to her.

— Ken and Margaret who have been involved since the beginning.

— Friends and colleagues at the University of Kent who have been so generous with their time and advice,

— and Alan Pryor who had the confidence to publish and who has been unstinting in his research and enthusiasm.

Jenifer K. Woods
Great-niece   1985

INTRODUCTION

It was originally intended to publish this diary in a simpler form but the idea has grown over the months. There are now more photographs and notes than were at first envisaged, in fact the research has become a very exciting development of the book.

For some reason Uncle Fred destroyed all his correspondence leaving only a few official documents and the diary.

The historical notes and explanations have been put under the day they refer to. Many of the photographs have come from private albums and have been reproduced often from small faded sepia prints.

Although it has been published much as it was written, it should be noted that a few minor adjustments were necessary to make the text easier to read.

The intention has been to build on the diary to give a wider view of events but no doubt there are many questions left unanswered.

ALAN PRYOR

ACKNOWLEDGEMENTS

The Publishers gratefully acknowledge the assistance of the following libraries and photographic libraries:

The Buffs Museum, Canterbury.

The Dargate Motor Museum, near Faversham, Kent.

The Imperial War Museum, London.

The Institution of Royal Engineers, Chatham, who supplied most of the photographs.

The Ministry of Defence Library, London.

The National Maritime Museum, London.

The R.A.F. Museum, Hendon.

The R.A.M.C. Historical Museum, Aldershot, Hants.

The Rotunder (The National Artillery Museum), Woolwich.

The Royal Artillery Institution, Woolwich.

The Small Arms Museum (The School of Infantry), Westminster.

No. 111 (F) Squadron, R.A.F., Fife, Scotland.

and the individuals who helped with the research, provided many details, or loaned photographs, postcards, or documents:

Lt. Col. Dick Bolton, R.A., for his valuable research.

Mrs. B. Brenner, "Seven Stones," Broadstairs, for details of the house.

Mr. and Mrs. W. E. Chandler of Broadstairs.

Dr. C. Church.

Dr. R. J. Crampton for his valuable knowledge and opinions.

Mr. S. Lutman for indexing the book.

Mr. Rodolf Matéjus for his personal experiences as a private in the Royal Norfolk Regiment. He joined up at the age of 16, having falsified his age, and served in the same area as Fred.

Col. G. W. A. Napier, R.E.

The Rev. E. J. Powe, Vicar of Holy Trinity Church, Broadstairs.

Messrs. E. and A. Robinson & Sons, Builders of Broadstairs — the successors of the firm of Jack May.

Dr. J. Whyman.

Mrs. Jenifer Woods for her co-operation and dedication in helping to produce this book.

Dr. D. Zancani.

LIST OF ILLUSTRATIONS

THE CAMPAIGN

The Great War of 1914 to 1918 was fought by the armies and navies of thirty-six nations across the globe from China to Argentina. Except for operations against the German colonies and at sea, campaigns of the War outside Europe were aimed directly or indirectly at Turkey. Turkey had formally joined Austria and Germany on 29th October 1914 and entered the war a month later.

On mobilisation, despite an ill-trained and ill-equipped army, Turkey set out to attack Russia in the Caucasus and the British in Egypt in addition to defending her long coast-line against possible British landings.

Egypt was nominally part of the Ottoman Empire but had been under British control since the building of the Suez Canal which was Britain's life-line to her Empire — the source of raw materials and reinforcements.

Early in 1915 Turkey attacked across the Sinai desert with two reinforced divisions, the aim twofold: to capture the Canal and evict the British from Egypt. The British defended the Canal with five half-trained divisions which were dug in on the West Bank and the result of 20,000 men attacking over an appreciable water obstacle against 70,000 dug-in defenders was not hard to predict. The unsuccessful Turks withdrew and for the remainder of 1915 the British continued to defend the Canal from the West Bank!

With little further activity in Egypt that year the British mounted two campaigns against the Turks, the first in Mesopotamia, the second in the Dardanelles: in Mesopotamia to protect the oil fields providing fuels for the Royal Navy and in the Dardanelles to divert Turkey from the Suez canal and keep them from reinforcing the Russian front. The disastrous Gallipoli campaign followed the Royal Navy's attack on the Dardanelles and an equally disastrous campaign was launched in Mesopotamia to capture Baghdad.

Meanwhile, Lawrence and his Arabs were disrupting Turkish lines of communication in Southern Arabia and it was not until the middle of 1916 that the British could reinforce Egypt in sufficient numbers to advance across the Sinai desert, backed by the sound logistic planning which had been lacking in Gallipoli and Mesopotamia.

The decision was then taken to advance into Palestine and capture Jerusalem which led to the first and second battles of Gaza and firmly established the British Expeditionary Force into Palestine, but with many casualties.

In June 1917 General Allenby relieved General Murray as the commander of the Force. By surprise and deception he captured first Beersheba and then Gaza and on the 8th December 1917 Jerusalem fell to the British, thus ending seven hundred years of Turkish control of the Holy City, the political effect of its capture far outweighing any military objective. Allenby's campaign was crowned in September 1918 by the battle of Megiddo, one of the best-planned and best-executed actions of World War I, and a month later Turkey requested an armistice. Her Palestine army was destroyed, the Salonika front had collapsed, her Mesopotamian forces were trapped, and from Aleppo to Mecca the Arabs were in revolt.

Lt. Col. DICK BOLTON R.A.

THE YEARS BEFORE

Frederick Thomas was born to George and Caroline Mills on 15th February 1883, the youngest of seven children: Adela, Alfred, Florence, Jess, Lily, William and Frederick. The family lived in Ramsgate, Kent, where most of the children were educated at St. George's School. Their father died in 1901 when Fred was 18.

George Mills
1840–1901.

Caroline Mills
1841–1928.

Fred joined the Volunteer force at Chatham barracks on 21st January 1901, the day that Queen Victoria died, and the Territorial Army in March 1913. He served as a Lance-Corporal for four years with the 4th Battalion The Buffs, his regimental number being 828.

Fred — aged 4, and brother Will aged 10.   *Fred aged about 14.*

Fred — third from the left, standing — as a Local Defence Volunteer.

Fred served an apprenticeship in the Isle of Thanet and became a master builder. In 1915 he worked for C.J. Attwood & Co. of King Street, Ramsgate and in 1917 was involved in the building of premises for the Royal Flying Corps in Dover, the contractors being Pickrills of Harrow.

Tradesmen who worked with Fred in Thanet.

Jessie

Fred

He was invited to be the best man at a wedding, and at the reception held in York Gate House, Broadstairs, he was introduced to one of the bridesmaids, Miss Jessie Heffer. She was five years younger and came from Wealdstone, Harrow where her father was also a builder. After their marriage they lived in Ramsgate and had a baby daughter who died in infancy.

Army Form E. 511.

If this Certificate is lost or mislaid no duplicate of it can be obtained.

DISCHARGE CERTIFICATE OF A SOLDIER OF THE TERRITORIAL FORCE.

This is to certify that (No.) _828_ (Rank) _Lce Corpl_

(Name) _Frederick Mills_

(Unit) _4th Bn The Buffs_

to serve in the Territorial Force of the County of _Kent_ who was enlisted

on the _twenty this_ day of _March_ 19/3,

and that his claims have been properly settled.

* is discharged in consequence of* _Engagement_

Termination of Engagement

His total service in the Territorial Force is _4_ years ___ days, including

Service abroad, viz., in _____ _____ years _____ days.

Medals, Clasps, and Decorations _____

(Signature of Officer Commanding Unit) _F. H. Keeler Lt._
n. Lieut. Colonel Co.
4th Batt'n. The Buffs.

(Place and Date) _Canterbury 4-4-19/3._

* Here state cause of discharge as detailed in the Regulations for the Territorial Force.

213   100,000   4—10   H W V   7 13 13   Forms E. 511   2

Telephone: 217 HARROW.

H. Pickrill,
Builder and Contractor.

24, CANNING ROAD,
WEALDSTONE,

Feb 27th 1917

Sir'

It affords us great pleasure to state that F. T. Mills has given us great satisfaction in the way in which he has carried out for us the erection & completion of Buildings for the Royal Flying Corps at Dover We believe he is a first class mechanic & straight-forward in his dealings with master, men & materials & would like him to work for us again when we again have work in his neighbourhood

Yours
H. Pickrill

One of his many references.

5

At the age of 34 he was called up and served in the 570 (Devon) Army Troop Company, Royal Engineers, on general construction work. The diaries which follow describe his experiences with the Egyptian Expeditionary Force from 1917 to 1920.

William, who served in the East Kent Regiment.

One of his brothers, William, served in France for most of the War.

THE DIARY
1917

Thursday, April 12th   Called up to Herne Bay and taken to Canterbury Barracks by motor. Medical Board, passed 'C1'. Posted to Royal Engineers at Chatham. Under canvas – snowing all night.

Friday, April 13th   Classification Insurance card posted to Mr. Cox. Regimental number 263445 P2 Company, Great Lines Camp.

Saturday, April 14th   Trade test – passed skilled 1/4 rating.

Wednesday, April 18th   Finally approved.

Thursday, April 19th   Vaccinated.

> Smallpox vaccination carried out in the UK – not compulsory.

R.A.M.C. Historical Museum

Monday, April 23rd   Drafted to 570th Works Company, Devon R.E(T) at Yatesbury, Wiltshire.

Fred sent this photograph to his mother in 1917.

Saturday, May 5th   Christchurch. Jumpers camp for course of field engineering.

Friday, June 15th   Inoculation – first dose.

Friday, June 22nd   Inoculation – second dose.

> Typhoid vaccination from 1915 (Triple vaccine for all British expeditionary forces – two injections 8 days apart).
>
> *R.A.M.C. Historical Museum*

Friday, July 13th   Leave for six days.

Friday, July 20th   'B2' raised to 'B1'

As from 1916. Category A

Men fit for general service. i.e. able to march, see to shoot, hear well, and stand active service conditions.
  i. Men fit for despatch overseas in all respects as regards training and physical and mental qualifications.
  ii. Recruits who should be fit for category AI when trained.
  iii. Men returned sick or wounded from an expeditionary force who should be fit for AI when hardened by work.
  iv. Recruits under 19 years of age.

Category C

Fit for service at home only, i.e. free from serious organic disease but only able to stand service conditions in garrisons at home.
  i. Any garrisons or provisional unit*
  ii. Any labour units or regimental outdoor employment†
  iii. On sedentary work as clerks, storemen, batmen, cooks, orderlies and on sanitary duties‡

Category E

Men unfit for service in Categories A, B or C and not likely to be fit within six months.

Category B

Men fit for service abroad but not for general service i.e. free from serious organic disease and able to stand service conditions on lines of communication in France or any garrison in the tropics.
  i. Any garrison or provisional units*
  ii. Any labour units or any garrison or regimental outdoor employment†
  iii. On sedentary work as clerks and storemen only‡

Category D

Men temporarily unfit for Categories A, B or C.
  i. In command depots.
  ii. In Regimental depots.
  iii. In any unit or depot under or awaiting medical or dental treatment.

*Men who could march at least 5 miles, see to shoot without glasses and hear well.
†Men able to walk not more than 5 miles to and from work and to see and hear sufficiently for ordinary purposes.
‡For men suitable for sedentary work only.

Medical Services General History vol. 1 HMSO 1921 by Maj. Gen. Sir W. G. MacPherson, K.C.M.G., C.B., LL.D.

Friday, August 3rd   Transferred to the 2nd/4th Devon R.E. Electric Light Company, Elphinstone Barracks, Plymouth. Going through a course of electricity for searchlight work.

Saturday, August 25th   Piers Cellars Battery, on Searchlight and Directing Station.

Wednesday, September 12th   Recalled to Elphinstone Barracks.

Thursday, September 13th   Transferred to 570th Army Troop Company, Devon R.E. at Cadford – warned for draft.

Friday, September 14th   Medical inspection – passed fit. All surplus kit returned; khaki drill, helmet and equipment issued.

Saturday, September 15th   Draft leave for six days.

Tuesday, September 18th Ramsgate. Will home from France − first meeting for three years.

One of his brothers, William (born in 1877) became a foreman for Dunns, the furniture removers of Ramsgate. He served with the East Kent Regiment in France for most of the War and had several lucky escapes when transporting goods to the line by pack mule.

Thursday, September 20th Back to Cadford.

Fred (third row, second from the right)
with other recruits − probably at Cadford.

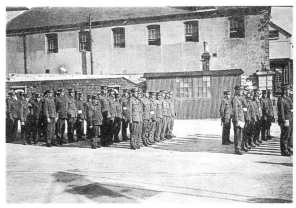

On parade.

Friday, September 21st Rifle and bayonet issued, also ground sheet and blanket.

Sunday, September 23rd Paybook and fifty rounds of ammunition issued.

Monday, September 24th Medical inspection − passed fit.

Wednesday, September 26th Rainy weather. Left Cadford for embarkation 1.10 p.m., arrived Southampton 3.30 p.m. Thousands of troops there − met 571st Devon R.Es − some of the old 30 party with them. Went on board the S.S. Caesarea, 700 mixed troops aboard, G106 was packed. Left Southampton 7.10 p.m. and The Roads, with escort, at 10.30 p.m. − good passage.

The S.S. Caesarea − 1,500 tons − was built in 1910 and owned by the London and South Western Railway Company.

Lloyd's Register 1917

SS Caesarea.   *National Maritime Museum*

Thursday, September 27th Arrived at Cherbourg, France, 4.30 a.m. and disembarked 7.30 a.m. Marched to Rest Camp No. 1, Army Post Office, S50, British Expeditionary Force, in a lovely park. Medical inspection — passed fit.

Friday, September 28th A lovely day. Left camp at 6.15 p.m. and entrained at the Gare Maritime three miles from camp. Started from there at 9.10 p.m. The train had to pass through streets for some distance — the people cheering as we passed. It was a bad permanent way with coaches which rocked and swung all over the place. An oil lamp for lighting. Six men to a compartment.

We passed Valognes and Caen then settled for the night, two on each seat, two on the floor. I slept on the floor with cap on top of boot for pillow, coat for blanket.

Saturday, September 29th Although shaken about had a good sleep and awoke at 6 a.m., misty but fine, sun shining. Drew up for five minutes at Alencon, French and British troops there. Had breakfast. Ten miles further on we stopped again at Le Mans — day's rations issued, bread, corned beef and tea. Le Mans is a big town and station with good buildings.

We then went through Vivion Beaumont and passed Saint Paterne; at all stations people seemed to expect us. They cheered and threw peaches, pears, apples etc. Many dropped on to the line but I managed to get peaches. We stopped at Tours, a large city with a big station junction — German prisoners there. We had a wash and tea. The last few miles have been lovely with detached mansions, vineyards, orchards and peaches growing wild. A very wide river or canal, nice bridges over it.

Our coach orderly officer handed round fags for the second time. Had a bit of supper and then got to bed on the floor at 9.15.

Sunday, September 30th   Awoke at 8 a.m., misty but fine. Passed through Gilly to Digoin – a lot of people on the station. More German prisoners there. The railway went round the side of a very steep hill. At Paray le Monial, another large station, I saw some big engines made of copper. We had breakfast and a wash.

We travelled upon the Paris, Lyon and Mediterranean Railway through hills and valleys. The railway went in and out of a range of mountains – the most lovely scenery I have ever seen. We arrived at St. Germain at 3 p.m. – people watched us at the station. Marched to Rest Camp No. 2 (Eastern) and spent the night in tents.

Monday, October 1st   Awoke at 6 a.m., had breakfast at St. Germain au Mont. Left at 3 p.m., 960 troops on board – one man left behind. A very hot day. We crossed a river with motor boats on it and passed a lovely pleasure park. French soldiers guarded bridges, tunnels and a big wireless station.

We came into a large city station like Euston – Lyon Brotteaux. French Red Cross nurses served us with a drink, I believe it was quinine. We stayed a long time at Lyon, the biggest city we have touched. The people crowded round us and cheered loudly.

We left the station the same way and branched off. Crossed the river again and passed Beynont, then a long range of mountains. A road and trees both sides for miles. Montluel. A flying school at the foot of the mountains. At Amberieu, we were issued with tea by the French soldiers. We passed the Schnapps' factory, Verieu-le-Grand and Guloz, a big station under the mountains. Arrived in Aix-le-Bains at 8.15 p.m.

Tea issued at 11.30 p.m. We have stopped here for one hour so as to cross the Italian frontier at 5 a.m. The last part of the journey has been through lovely mountains, valleys, rivers, lakes and villages. A full moon made it beautiful. All cafés lighted up and busy. We are close to Mont Blanc – I hope to see it. All the troops are singing for the benefit of the French people who are here to see us. The houses in this district are built upon the Swiss style – some nearly up to the top of the mountains.

Tuesday, October 2nd   Didn't have any sleep, the scenery was so grand in the moonlight. Crossed a lovely river and saw several waterfalls. Passed Mont Blanc at 2.05 a.m. The mountains are very steep and high. All ground is planted at the foot. Another lovely river breaking on the rocks with the moonlight catching it. Crossed the Italian frontier at Modane at 6 a.m.

Changed trains, have now got a 1st class carriage – plush seats and lace headrests. Had a splendid wash – I wanted it! This station has a river alongside and mountains all round with forts on top. This has opened my eyes, how valleys come between such great hills with only room for railway and river. There are electric trains here, an overhead system, water powered. Have just seen an Algerian soldier – red breeches and cap, khaki coat. Italian soldiers also have nice uniforms. Now going for breakfast.

Left Modane at 10 a.m. Sun is quite hot – gets more so each day, but snow still on the peaks of the mountains. It took forty minutes to get through a long mountain tunnel with air shafts at intervals. Lovely cascades from the mountains, the peaks capped with snow were above the clouds. Lakes of clear green water at the bottom. Artistic houses all around. Train stopped – the brakes had got hot – had water from brook.

Have just had dinner. Bought large pears, three a penny, and a long loaf for 9d. – that was a treat. We have been coming down hill since Modane through a lovely gorge all the way, it is a sight never to be forgotten. Where the train is now standing the mountains disappear in the clouds on both sides. There are wooden houses dotted about all over them. How the people get up and down I can't imagine. There are plots cultivated and cows grazing on the hills.

At 2.25 p.m. stopped at Susa – bought a nice bunch of black grapes for 2d. Saw a castle on the highest mount and a white obelisk on another. Train stopped a while in Moncalieri at 5 p.m. so had a water bottle shave and tea by the rails. Milano − the country is now flat but pretty, oxen drawing carts along the roads or ploughing. Electricity is distributed all over the country although it seems countrified. Carts with great barrels of wine going past drawn by two horses with white hoods on. The railways in both France and Italy seem to be a public thoroughfare, people walk along and across the lines at will, children get on footboard and ride sometimes. A big town now, a river with bridges over it. A big church with a dome, and a lot of big buildings. The largest café and casino about Villafranca-d'Asti and main station Asti Alessandria 8 p.m.

Wednesday, October 3rd Awoke 6 a.m. − had a good night's rest. We are now in a fruit-growing district with vineyards. The vines are never more than four feet high then spread out. Electric trams.

Reached Faenza 9 a.m. They call it a rest camp but we are working all the time and not allowed out into the town. We can get a large bunch of white grapes for a cigarette. Wore our helmets today for the first time. All wine carts are painted with pictures, some drawn by eight oxen. We can get lovely bread, white and new, best I've had since the war started. Some nice pottery here. Had breakfast, dinner and tea then had to scrub all the tables, forms and floor. The tents are double ones to protect soldiers from the heat of the day and dampness by night.

Entrained at 7.45 p.m. and started off again at 9 p.m.

Thursday, October 4th Awoke at 5.30 a.m. − passing Potenza Picena. On the left of train is the Adriatic Sea quite close. Fishing boats, nets, bathing huts. On the right a range of hills with towns on them. Pedaso at 7 a.m., a lighthouse and signalling station. Sea is very calm, some people bathing. Grottammare, a swell place with lovely painted houses, trees in the streets and parks. Some guns on the seashore manned by Italian sailors who are quartered in railway cars with big awnings over them. Porto D'Ascoli, palms and bigger vines here. Men, women and children work in the fields barefooted.

No food since 4 p.m. yesterday, it is now 9 a.m., getting very hungry. As water will be short we have a two-gallon can full in our compartment. We had breakfast at Castellamare Adriatico and drew the day's rations − eighteen hours since our last meal. All sorts of fruit dirt cheap. We have just been for a bathe, it was lovely. Sands for miles, quite a seaside resort. Noon − a bit hot but I like it. Two quinine pills taken.

Train started off again at 1.15 p.m. − guns on railway trucks. We passed Torina de Sangro − lighthouse on the headland. Stopped at Termoli, junction for Naples − French and English money refused. Aircraft guns and forts here.

Tea issued at Foggia at 10.30 p.m. − got out of bed to drink it.

Friday, October 5th Left Foggia 12.30 a.m. I awoke at 6 a.m. passing Bari, a lovely town. All the houses are white and have mosquito nets over doors and windows. Rare lot of cactus plants about here, my old friends. There are miles of old olive trees, the trunks are split and twisted − they look hundreds of years old with stone piers built under to keep them up. Just sighted the first ship, a destroyer patrolling the coast of Ostuna. Very stony ground here with a lot of aloe bushes ten feet high.

We stopped at Brindisi at 11 a.m. for breakfast and rations issue of one box of matches, two packets of cigarettes, one ounce bar of tobacco. Departed at 1.30 p.m., not much coal here, wood is largely used for engines. Nice domes shining in the sunlight, stone quarries with grottos in them.

Saw aeroplanes at Grottaglie station.

Arrived at Taranto at 8.30 p.m. − detrained in the dark. Had a job to get to tents. Detachments have been waiting five weeks here for boat. It rained, the first we have had since crossing the Channel. Had a drop of tea and went to bed in double tents. No boards, but mud inside.

Saturday, October 6th Awoke at 6 a.m. had breakfast at 8.30. Tea, bread, marmalade, Gillards' service rations. Lizards and mosquitoes here. Taranto is a big port, warships in the harbour and large works. Coolies who are singing all the time. We are under double canvas tents but they are building large stone cookhouses etc. Dinner – meat, canned vegetables, stewed tea, brand and Libby's veal loaf. Inoculated and at 6 p.m. had a dose of quinine. Got some tent boards.

An Italian destroyer off Taranto.   *Institution of Royal Engineers*

Sunday, October 7th Sunday Divine service at 8.30 a.m. We are to wear drills and helmets now. Hope to leave here soon as it is a chronic camp and only half finished. Had a washing day, the first time I have had to wash my own things. Have hung them on trees – they won't be long drying as it's nice and hot. We are known here as the No. 41 train party.

Monday, October 8th This place is being built by Italians for a naval base. We had a swim in the Gulf of Taranto. Usual camp fatigues. Fine day, very hot.
   A battery of English artillery with guns arrived from the Italian front going to Egypt.

Tuesday, October 9th Lovely day. About 2,000 troops left the camp for Egypt. We were on camp fatigues.

Wednesday, October 10th More artillery arrived from the Italian front. Camp fatigues. Shifted from tents to Cimino camp into huts which are more healthy. Received letters from home, the first since leaving Cadford – it was a treat.

Thursday, October 11th   Camp fatigues etc. More troops gone to Egypt. Issued with mosquito nets, one between two men. Some officers arrived from torpedoed transport sunk off Crete.

Have been watching the lightning which is pretty although terrible should it touch anything. They call it "Wild Fire" here. Keeps in the same spot due East.

Friday, October 12th   First night under the mosquito net. Very nice, not troubled at all. Had rain during the night but fine now. Y.M.C.A. opened for tea and biscuits. Great success.

Saturday, October 13th   Awoke early, so cold I could not sleep again. Packed up baggage of officers going on leave, hammock chairs among it. There is not much twilight here, but very starlit.

Notice given that seventeen bags of mail for us went down in the Channel by act of enemy on the 10th.

Sunday, October 14th   Very cold night again. Two long troop trains just come in, camp nearly full. Camp fatigues. Vicar of Christchurch Priory arrived for Salonica.

Monday, October 15th   Ordered to be ready to embark tomorrow. Shall be very pleased to get away from here, it is very unhealthy and getting worse. The rate of change of money varies. At present the value of an English shilling is 1 lire 75 centisimi, or 1.75. Ten lire is 5/8d. Troop trains came in late.

Tuesday, October 16th   Sgt. Major awoke us at 5 a.m. We are to parade with kit bags at 6.30 ready for embarkation at 8 a.m.

We embarked at Marconi pier on to an iron barge. Had to go below – it was terrible, so stuffy and packed although only 15 minutes journey. Several fainted. We then got on board the P. & O. boat Kashmir. It is a fine boat but we are again packed, about 2,000 troops and about 100 officers. The officers have state rooms and as much deck space as the 2,000. It is terribly hot below and no room on deck. It's a disgrace after over three years' experience – we are not allowed here or there.

We left Taranto harbour at 4.30 p.m., with two Japanese destroyers and two British as escort. Italian ships were manned and cheered as we passed out. I was on submarine guard, about fifty of us with fifty rounds of ammunition each. Two hours on, four off, but no place to lie down.

> The P. & O. Kashmir – 8,841 tons – was built by Laird & Company of Greenock in 1915. She was 480 feet in length, had three decks and sailed under a British flag.
>
> *Lloyds Register 1917*

Wednesday, October 17th   Been up all night, a bit rough at times but fine. We have been going SE by S. At 6 a.m. we went east. We sighted Corfu at 1 p.m., on the port side, then went south passing a lot of islands. Passed a drifting mine. We had a practise call to quarters – hopeless confusion. We, who were quartered in the stern had to go up to the bow; those in the bow had to come to the stern. God help us if anything does happen.

The sea is a very deep blue like Reckitts blue, so different from our green. The sun went down so suddenly. I could see it going. It got dark quickly then. Nowhere to lie down, the grass in our garden would be acceptable much less a bed.

Thursday, October 18th   Managed to have a good sleep although the ship rocked a bit. Many went up on deck so I slept on the table with a lifebelt as a pillow. They are very particular about lifebelts, we wear them all the time. Sighted land at 6 a.m. on the starboard bow – looks like a desolate mountain. Time has just advanced one hour.

We have entered Suda Bay, Crete, and dropped anchor in a land-locked harbour with

P. & O. Kashmir. *National Maritime Museum*

high hills that have forts on them. Several British warships and merchantmen in here — we are today flying the Red Ensign. Quite a good sized town, but no cultivation. Ground is all rock.

We must not smoke after dark, that's about 5 p.m. because of it being seen on deck. The officers come out of their mess room smoking and a strong light goes across the sea every time the door opens. Down below we are packed with shells.

Boats came around with grapes, apples, pears, etc. We were stopped from buying them by the officers saying they were bad for us owing to fever but about half an hour afterwards they bought tons for themselves! They have now gone ashore, they are having a fine time. We are staying in here tonight and officers from the destroyers have come on board — for a beano, I expect.

Friday, October 19th   I managed to sleep on the table again last night. One chap fell out of his hammock on to me, but that is small trouble. The Corporal of the guard woke me up twice because he thought I was one of his party.

We left Suda Bay at 8 a.m., kept close to land for a long way sailing SE with land on the starboard side. We kept along the north side of Crete and saw a lot of the Grecian islands. The hospital on the ship is full and everybody has a severe cold.

There are very particular about lights and belts now. This is the most dangerous part. There are artillery on board with guns and 80,000 shells so there would not be much chance for us if we did get hit.

A sea mine washed ashore near Jaffa. Note the horns which are wire cages containing bottles of acid which make contact when broken.
Institution of Royal Engineers

Saturday, October 20th   Slept on the table again. Got up early and saw the sunrise. It's lovely here. I don't find it too hot but there is an awful smell down below, enough to poison us. In peacetime there are about 1,000 people on board. All told there are now 3,000 so one can understand what it is like. I think we are out of danger now. Just seen a sailing ship, the first we have passed all the way.

Sighted Egypt at 12.05 noon. Different sort of country than that we have passed. We stopped and an English steam trawler brought a pilot aboard. We all had to put on lifebelts and stay on deck whilst going through the minefield before entering Alexandria harbour. A lot of English ships here, the sea is green like at home. There are a lot of English firms with workshops on the docks. Alexandria is a big place — the buildings are fine and large with domes or flat roofs.

We disembarked at 5 p.m. and went straight to a train. The officers have all been across to cable but there is no chance for us to do so. We are packed in horrible carriages again with shutters here and there instead of windows. We left Alexandria at 6 p.m. and travelled in the dark, passing through Zagazig and Ismailia.

Sunday, October 21st   Had no sleep last night, hardly room to sit down. We arrived at Kantara at 3 a.m. — got out of the train at 5 a.m. We are close to the Suez Canal. There are several bridges across the Canal built on iron barges some of which are movable to let ships pass. Whilst in the station one big vessel went through. Some native sailing boats were on the Canal which is not very wide.

We crossed the Canal about 6 a.m. to a big camp. Miles and miles of tents, thousands of motor lorries. Nothing but sand here. This is a rest camp and hospital for the Turkish front. We have had a good breakfast and dinner, it's quite a treat celebrating Sunday. I shall try the Officer Commanding to get a cablegram off.

We shifted to our own camp close to the Canal. We bathed in the Canal and went across the bridge to the Australian canteen. I had a pint of coffee and big plate of trifle for 3 piastres. There are plenty of eggs but they are small. I enquired about the 2nd/24th London Regiment — they were here but have now gone up to the front. I may see some here later, I should like to meet Stan to have a chat.

Monday, October 22nd We were not allowed to cable. Just as I thought, the officers' wives must know, but ours — well! They don't think they are the same people. On top of that the mail leaves here every Monday, letters have to be in on Saturday so it means being here a week before we can get a letter off.

A lot of wounded came from the front today in motors and were put on a Red Cross train. More ships have gone up and down the Canal today. They have a big light on the bow at night to enable them to see the banks.

Tuesday, October 23rd Some of the Company have been detailed for work, some in charge of natives. I had a swim in the Suez Canal. This place is close to where the Australians fought the Turks and drove them from the Canal. A lot of infantry went up to the line today. The Captain has gone to Cairo.

Had a good supper tonight, eggs with bread and butter. It was a bit like home but the eggs were cheaper, four for 5d.

Troops were concentrating for the attack on Beersheba.

History of the Great War — Military Operations Egypt and Palestine

Mess huts at Kantara built by Anzac Field Squadron. *Institution of Royal Engineers*

Wednesday, October 24th On camp fatigues etc.

Thursday, October 25th Changed a £1 note for Egyptian money. Its value was 97½ Pt. A lot more troops arrived.

Friday, October 26th Troopship arrived in the Canal close to us from India. Some Territorials came ashore. Six Japanese destroyers went up the Canal towards the Mediterranean.
  Pay day.

> Japan declared war on Germany on 23rd August 1914 after she refused to withdraw her warships from Chinese and Japanese waters and surrender the German-leased territory of Kiao-Chiao to China. When it fell on 7th November 1914 Japan assumed administration of the territory.
>   Japanese squadrons were sent to the China Sea and the Pacific and Atlantic oceans. They also performed convoy duty in the Mediterranean protecting allied vessels. Several actions took place against German submarines. Over 700 allied ships are thought to have been successfully escorted. No Japanese troops were sent to Europe.
>
> *Encyclopaedia Britannica 14 ed Vol 14   Naval Notes 1914–1918 Naval Attache British Embassy Tokyo*

Sugi – in British waters, note the washing on a line between funnels.   *National Maritime Museum*

Sugi – launched 1915 the first Japanese designed destroyer. Speed 30 knots, one 4.7" Q.F. four 3.2 guns., four 18" tubes above water. Twelve were built for the French Navy.   *Janes Fighting Ships*

Saturday, October 27th They have just taken letters for censor, hope they go soon. Three Japanese destroyers gone up the Canal.

A 13 pounder 9 cwt. Q.F. A.A. gun mounted on a 40 h.p. chain driven Peerless Troup Carrying lorry.

Royal Artillery Institution

The same lorry as above – with unloading problems!   *Royal Artillery Institution*

Entries in captured diaries of the enemy flying corps headquarters and squadrons show that machines were continually being damaged and reconnaissances prevented by anti-aircraft fire. The following are typical extracts.

"20/3/18. Machines hit at Ramlen at height of 4,700 metres"

"13 – 19/4/18. Anti-aircraft defence still very strong and makes things difficult for our working machines in reconnaissances"

"19/7/18. Machine of 300 Squadron was seriously damaged in the elevator by anti-aircraft hits. Glided down to 500 metres and broke up on the ground.   *A brief record of the Advance of the E.E. Force 1917–1918*

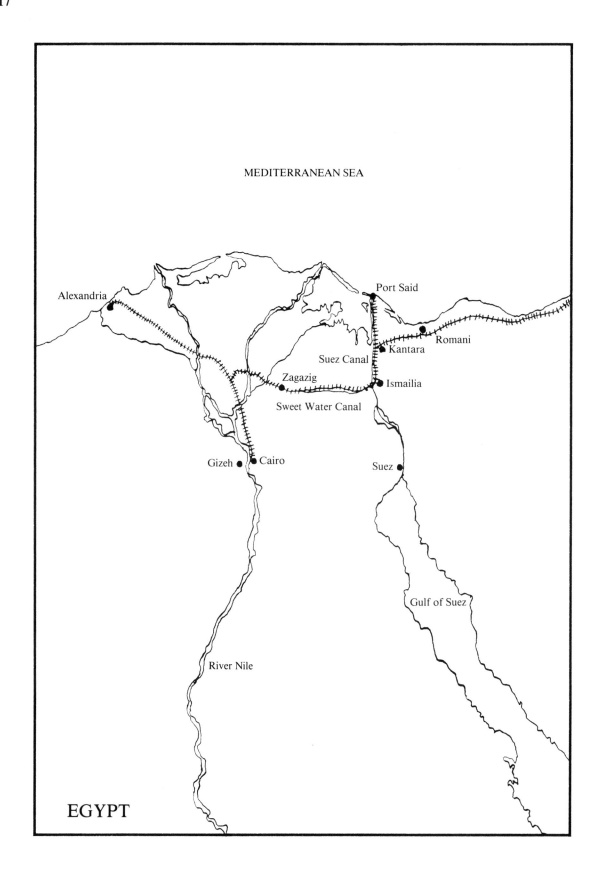

MEDITERRANEAN SEA

Alexandria

Port Said

Romani

Kantara

Suez Canal

Zagazig

Ismailia

Sweet Water Canal

Gizeh ● ●Cairo

Suez ●

Gulf of Suez

River Nile

EGYPT

Sunday, October 28th   Letters from home, first to get here. Some newspapers as well.

Monday, October 29th   Lots of wounded came down today.

  The band of the Rifle Brigade came and gave a concert in the canteen at 3 p.m. Started with ''Land of Hope and Glory'' then all popular songs; it quite livened things up. I thought of Wellington Gardens, a hammock chair and a cigar.

MkI Ordnance Q.F. (Quick Firing) 13 pounder 9 cwt on a MkI mounting. A very early form of air defence.

Institution of Royal Engineers

Tuesday, October 30th   Camp fatigues. Listened to the band in the evening.

Wednesday, October 31st   Letters and papers from home. A lot of anti-aircraft on lorries gone up today; wounded coming down. I have been at work upon our permanent camp making things as comfortable as possible. Issued with knickers.

Beersheba captured. British casualties − 167 killed, 1,042 wounded and five missing.

History of the Great War

Turkish prisoners at Beersheba.

Institution of Royal Engineers

Sunday, November 4th   Shifted the camp to a better ground. It is terrible to see the wounded coming down from the line but they have done well. A lot of prisoners captured at Beersheba came in today. They were a wretched lot, all ages, some without boots, with all sorts of clothing on.

Have heard of several train loads of British troops stopped in Italy for their front. They were to come here.

Turkish captured: 70 officers, 1,450 other ranks.

History of the Great War

Tuesday, November 6th   Our ammunition had to be returned to store. A lot of wounded Turks gone through to the station.

Wednesday, November 7th   Gaza taken but oh! the wounded. It's awful. A lot of English nurses have arrived today, the first white women I have seen for some time. We are in the desert.

This was the third battle of Gaza; the others were on March 26th 1917 and April 19th 1917.

History of the Great War − Military Operations Egypt and Palestine

Friday, November 9th   Hundreds of Turkish prisoners have come down, some were old men with white whiskers and some quite boys. If they had uniforms they were German, but most had any sort they had been able to get. All were in rags. Quite a number of officers, Austrian and German among them. Our wounded keep coming down.

Hundreds of horses, mules and donkeys, poor things. Some were wounded but all were starving, the worst horses I have ever seen. They could hardly walk to the Remount Depot. They will get looked after there.

Turkish prisoners at Kantara.   *Institution of Royal Engineers*

Over 1,000 prisoners were captured during 9th–10th November. Figures supplied by the Historical Section of the Turkish General Staff are from 31st October to 31st December 1917 and amounted to 28,443:

	Killed	Wounded	Missing
Officers	181	394	464
Other ranks	3,387	9,021	14,996

British casualties as reported weekly to Whitehall from week-ending 3rd November 1917 to 15th December 1917 were as follows:

	Killed	Wounded	Missing
Officers	203	807	32
Other ranks	2,306	13,391	1,689

The loss of British horses, mules and donkeys from 31st October to 31st December 1917 amounted to 10,000 including battle casualties.

History of the Great War – Military Operations Egypt and Palestine

Monday, November 12th   Taken charge of a new water filtering plant in course of construction. There are two contractors: The Cairo Water Company who are doing the machinery and main pipes, and an Italian firm doing the building. There are Italian and French foremen and some of the Egyptian Labour Corps. I have to supervise all work and

Turkish troops with German 7.92 mm 1908 model Maxim machine guns.   Institution of Royal Engineers

report to an officer the number of men employed and nature of work. It is a job to understand and to be understood. The works are on the bank of the Suez Canal at Kantara.

> The Regimental war diary actually quotes Sapper Mills taking charge here − it was most unusual for a private soldier to be mentioned.

Thursday, November 15th   Another officer has taken the job in hand and sent more sappers of 360 Company to help me dam the Sweet Water Canal which runs close alongside the Suez Canal.

Sunday, November 18th   Six of our Company have gone to Gaza. They are engine drivers from the Light Company. Thousands of prisoners have passed here this last day or so − Turks, Bulgarians, Germans and Austrians. Good number of officers well guarded.

Bread and marmalade for a Sunday dinner! What a treat! Had five minutes' rain today.

Monday, November 19th   We had a cyclonic storm at 2.40 p.m. Thunder and lightning first, then a big black cloud came up with an awful wind which took off the roofs of huts. Some were shifted altogether. Thousands of tents blown some distance. Our blankets and kit were left all over the place, wet through with the rain which descended in sheets. Never seen the likes before. We were all wet through and not a dry rag of any kind to put on. A large tract of the desert was like a lake. When we got home from work we had to find our kit and put our tent up in miserable rain. I had a good night on the waterproof sheet.

Tuesday, November 20th   Miserable day and a bit colder so put on serge suit again. The poor natives were too cold to work. They wrapped themselves up in their blankets and crawled into corners out of the wind, whilst I was running about in shirt sleeves. Got some things dry.

The remains of a Mk. 1 female tank from the first battle of Gaza. It was afterwards used as an observation post by the Turks and was shelled by the British.   *Institution of Royal Engineers*

The first British tank was the Mark I. Built in two types — "male" and "female" — both had sponsors mounted on the side to carry the main armament. On the male tank this consisted of two six-pound guns and on the female four Vickers' machine guns. The Mark I was 26 feet long, weighed 28 tons and had a crew of eight. Maximum speed was 4 m.p.h.; both types carried sufficient petrol to cover fifteen miles. Seventy-five of each were built in 1916.

Encyclopaedia Britannica 14 Ed.

Wednesday, November 21st   Lovely day, sun shining, everything drying up nicely as it is hot again.

Sunday, November 25th   Got a day pass for Ismailia. Started from camp 9 a.m. and caught the 9.20 train from Kantara. Return fare 6 Pt. Arrived at Ismailia after a fifty-minute journey across the sand. By the Suez Canal there is a fine station and a road runs directly in front of it for a long way with tall palm trees on each side. At the end is the Salt Water Lake with a small jetty going out into it. Motor boats and yachts and quite a little harbour. Along the bank of the lake is a lovely park called the Wilderness. Trees, cactus, flowers of all sorts and *grass!* The first grass I have seen here. The flowers were lovely, funny to see them in November. A lot of people in the park, mostly European and Jews, some playing tennis. There is quite a nice quarter for them with fine roads and houses. The shops were open and nearly all understood English. Bought Christmas presents at an Indian shop.

The native quarter was a collection of mud huts in a filthy condition. Fowls, ducks, turkeys, pigs all in the hut with the people. Tons of sugar canes about, sold in the street from barrows. They break them across their knee and chew them from the middle. The shops were awfully dirty.

We had our food at an Australian canteen, a lovely place out in the open under the palms. The cakes were just like Benoits in peacetime. Cream cakes and fancy cakes with icing all over. I thought how different it was at home, plenty of sugar here.

Caught the 9.25 p.m. for Kantara arriving in camp 10.20 p.m. after a most enjoyable day.

Benoits was a Belgian cake-shop back home.

A day pass to Ismailia. (Reduced in size)   Royal Artillery Institution

Sunday, December 2nd   Sunday working, just the same as other days. Breakfast – a small rissole of corned beef, bread, pint of tea. Dinner consisted of one pint of tea, two tablespoons of boiled rice and bread. Tea – a slice of meat, bread, tea. Lucky to get that.

Party with tool carts arrived.

Monday, December 3rd   Another blanket issued. Very glad of it as it is cold at night.

Friday, December 7th   Returned sun helmet to store, discarded the knickers and put on serge clothing again. It is just comfortably warm with them.

Saturday, December 8th   Completed job at filter plant and cleaned out fresh water canal. Food is very scarce now.

Sunday, December 9th   Church parade but no Minister appeared so were dismissed. First issue of soap. Very cold last night but hot again now. Dinner – curried corned beef, potatoes, dates.

Wednesday, December 12th   Saw a lot of captured Turkish guns on rail for Cairo. Some looked nearly new.

Friday, December 14th   Where I am at work there are turnips, carrots, beetroot and cabbage plants just coming through the ground. Broad beans in bloom, French beans 6″ high, tomatoes ripening in the open. Sunflowers in full bloom and a few potatoes. They dug some for dinner, they looked lovely, that was my share.

Sunday, December 16th   Sunday working. Issue of margarine, the first we have had in Egypt. Quite a treat.

Tuesday, December 18th Had a little rain today but sun is not quite so hot. Received the parcel sent by mother.

Thursday, December 20th Saw the S.S. Minnetonka go down the Canal with troops and a lot of nurses on board.

> The SS Minnetonka – 13,528 tons – was built by Harland and Wolff Ltd. of Belfast in 1902. She was 607 feet in length and had four decks. Owned by Atlantic Transport Co. Ltd. she sailed under a British flag. She would have been an impressive sight in the narrow confines of the Canal.
>
> *Lloyds Register 1917*

SS Minnetonka. *National Maritime Museum*

Friday, December 21st The parcel from Lyons Oxford Street sent by Jessie arrived quite safe and sound. Boiled chicken, Christmas pudding and cake all in sealed tins so am alright for a Christmas dinner.

Monday, December 24th The sun is shining but a very high wind is blowing the sand in clouds. It cuts the face and eyes something awful. The sand is so thick in the wind that it is not possible to see far.

Tuesday, December 25th, Christmas Day 1917 Reveille at 5.30 a.m. Wash and shave, breakfast at 6 a.m. Work at 7 a.m., ceased at noon. There was a hawker near the station with a stall selling cauliflowers, greens, *green peas,* oranges, nuts, figs, fish, bread, eggs and most lovely roses.

Captured German guns.
12 cm Howitzers designed by Krupp — were made in Essen in small numbers and also in the Putiloy Arsenal.

Institution of Royal Engineers

We had dinner at 12.30. There was a bit of Christmas pudding for each man. In the afternoon there was a football match. Tea at 4.30 p.m. — tea, bread, jam, cake, mince pie; extras were bought out of Company funds. At dinnertime I opened the pudding from home. It was a splendid relish. Suppertime the cake from home — that was the same. It has been a lovely day. At 7 a.m. it was just like a spring morning, sun shining and a nice breeze blowing but it got hot later. I thought of home all day.

Wednesday, December 26th, Boxing Day   Reveille at 5.30 a.m., work as usual. Midday meal — bread and cheese issue, cake from home. Dinner at 5 p.m. — meat and rice, cheese. After supper I had boiled chicken from home. Cigars and oranges very cheap — one, two and four cigars for 1 Pt. Two and three oranges for 1 Pt.

Friday, December 28th   Got a day off with a pass for Port Said — return fare 8½ Pt. Caught 11.10 a.m. train, about one hour's run. The rail runs alongside Suez Canal all the way. Passed two Suez Canal Signal stations, Tineh and Rao el Eich.

Port Said is a big place with a lot of shipping and docks. The inhabitants appeared to be mostly French and a few English. Some young fellows too, no doubt from the dockyard. It has a long sea front with bathing huts, large hotels and casinos. The good streets had shops like London but taking the town right through it is a dirty place and full of Chinese. The only trams were drawn by mules. Anyone could walk as fast so it must be only lazy people riding. I left again at 6.30 p.m.

Saturday, December 29th   Cut myself at work on a 6″ water main which had broken close to Hill 70, twenty kilometres from Kantara, right in the desert. Only break there is to be seen here are the old trenches and breastworks that the Australians fought behind. Sandbags, broken harness, carts; all sorts of wreckage here. They are taking away the barbed wire for use further up. We came on a motor lorry.

Turkish colour party.   *Institute of Royal Engineers*

Captured German guns.   *75 mm*   *77 mm*
Germany began to build these guns in 1895 and the 75mm was still being used in World War II. They were made in many countries.   *Institution of Royal Engineers*

Fred fifth from the right
– outside the canteen at Kantara.

1918

Tuesday, January 1st   We worked until 12 noon. In the afternoon we had base sports with some good races etc, among them a mule race. Very funny as they wouldn't pass each other so started and finished together. Then a camel race – they ran faster than horses and were so awkward that it was wonderful how the riders could keep on their backs. It was a lovely day and quite hot.

Sunday January 13th   Civilian Egyptians are being taught to drive motor lorries, etc. to replace the drivers of the Army Service Corps. who are transferred to infantry. Thousands of Turkish prisoners are also working here now.

The Egyptian Labour Corps are paid thus

Labourers	5 Pt. per day
Mechanics	12 Pt. per day
Army Sergeants	£8 to £13 per month
Corporals	£2 to £6 month
Motor drivers and cooks	500 Pt. per month

The Egyptian Labour Corps was recruited from the local population to enable a pool of labour to be established at various centres.

As the E.L.C. expanded many officers were recruited from the ranks of British units and given temporary commissions. They had to learn Arabic and be able to supervise Egyptians; each officer had charge of 200 men. A company was made up of twelve gangs of 50 men, with some skilled personnel attached.

In 1916 the E.L.C. was sent to France (10,403), Mesopotamia (8,280) and Salonica (600). By November 1918 the strength of the E.L.C. reached 100,002 with 504 officers.

Joining up 12" pipes at Salmana Sinai.   *Institution of Royal Engineers*

Fred (Wearing hat) with E.L.C.

Monday, January 14th   Working at the Greek Sisters' quarters at 44th Stationary Hospital laying 4″ water main for fire appliances. The first English women I have spoken to since leaving home.

Wednesday, January 16th   Two sappers, one native fitter and twenty-five naffers completed laying and covering 1560 ft. of 4″ pipe and ten tees in twenty-two hours − the trench was 18″ deep in hard sand.

We had the afternoon off for a football final between Royal Ordnance Depot and Base Hospital. Base Hospital won one-nil.

Sunday, January 20th   Got a day pass to Port Said. Had a splendid time, dinner and tea at an English hotel kept by Mr. D. Sams, a Man of Kent whose home was at Gillingham. For tea we had a large fried sole and chipped potatoes − lovely − a tenth the price of fish at home. English beer 1/5d. a quart bottle. A lot of places "out of bounds".

Friday, February 1st   A native digging 30 yards outside our workshop dug up a Mills bomb. He started to find out what it was and pulled out the pin and off it went. Pieces rattled against the iron of the shop. We sent him to hospital, I don't fancy he will be able to play with another. This is the second bomb dug up in a fortnight, the last one injured eight men badly. A lot of bayonets and rifle ammunition also dug up.

Monday, February 4th   Very cold early in the day, heavy hailstorm at 9.30 a.m. Hailstones quite one inch in size. I was in the workshop under an iron roof, the noise was awful. Horses ran away in all directions; it lasted about twenty minutes then the sun came out and was hot. Just before the storm there came clouds of flies and mosquitoes. A lot of tents and huts blown down.

Three more natives injured, one killed by a bomb they had found and were playing with behind the Mosque. There seem to be a lot about somewhere.

Thursday, February 7th   Started setting out casings for engine and pump beds, 4.90 h.p. engines to force water to Romani.

Sunday, February 10th   There are great preparations for another advance. Field kitchens, water carts, motors and guns. Men, also, are continually passing through.

A lot of cold wind this last day or so, a little rain.

Monday, February 11th   Volunteers asked for to go away and do a very dangerous job. Don't know what it is but we don't understand Arabic good enough for that sort of work.

Saturday, February 16th   A sand storm came on about 8 p.m. and continued late into the night. It was bad for the eyes. I got right under the blankets but the sand found its way everywhere.

Monday, February 18th   Got a day pass to Zagazig − two hours' journey. Return fare 20 Pt. It was a nice day and we went through a lot of cultivated land. Sugar cane growing and all sorts of vegetables. It was a treat to see green fields. Zagazig is a big native town and a busy place. Saw all sorts of work going on − blacksmiths, wheelwrights, wood turning. Iron trunks, bedsteads and furniture were being made. The place has electric light and a little park. Rather pretty birds and animals in cages and the Egyptian Police Band playing ordinary tunes in the stand. Heard someone say ''go to mother'' − the voice came from behind the bushes. I said, ''that sounds strange'' then an Englishman and two ladies with a pretty child came and spoke to us.

Wednesday, February 20th   Taken away from 360th Water Company and put under one of my own officers in charge of building Indian Base Depot − a rare lot of buildings in mud brick. Started with ten carpenters, ten bricklayers, fifty labourers; expect two hundred tomorrow.

Thursday, February 21st   Inoculation against cholera. Issued with green goggles for protection of the eyes during sandstorms etc.

Saturday, February 23rd   French mortar school started practise close at hand. Several pieces blew back among us on the job but no one was hit. Reported it to our officer. No notice taken.

Monday, February 25th   French mortar practise again, more natives cleared off. Officer came on job and had a narrow escape. A corporal and myself got behind the brickstack and it was lucky we did. The officer went off and had it stopped at once. It is alright now.

Sunday, March 3rd   Rations cut down ten per cent. If they cut it down any more we shall have to give some back that we have already had. Hardly enough to exist upon now.

Tuesday, March 5th   Captured two Arabs. They said they had walked from Jerusalem in twenty days so they were handed over to the police. I can't imagine how they were at large.

Thursday, March 7th   Indian labour started work on the camp, two hundred of 121st Pioneers Regiment. They are far worse than the Egyptians, they have no idea of building and move so slowly between the two lots it's an awful job. I can now make the natives understand and some speak English but the Indians don't and I know not a word.

Saturday, March 9th   An Egyptian Labour Corps private shot at 6 a.m. for killing an English Egyptian Labour Corps officer. All the E.L.C. paraded to see it done.

Have had an awful day with Gippos and Indians, the Indians don't work fast enough to keep themselves warm. Even here they have a piper playing to them whilst at work. Scotch and Irish songs − have just finished ''The Wearing of the Green''.

We now have some of the City Imperial Yeomanry working here as labourers. One chap comes from Warrington Road, Harrow.

Sunday, March 10th   Some Buffs here for work today but none that I know. Artillery, Middlesex, Northampton, Sussex all mixed up. General Broadbent, Inspector of the Indian Labour Corps, inspected job.

Monday, March 11th   Twelve of the Royal Bucks Hussars reported to me for work − pick and shovel. Not a mechanic among them − they don't like work.

Tuesday, March 12th   Three hundred of the Sikh Pioneers 230th Regiment now working on the job. A corporal has been sent up to the job now that it is all set out.

Friday, March 15th   Rough day, first a sandstorm. I was right away from shelter. It was wicked. Then thunder, lightning and rain.

Saturday, March 16th   High wind and rain. It's almost the finish of the winter as they call it here.

Extra 6d. per day has been put in pay book as from September 29th. Compulsory allotment now done away with.

Twelve men sent to me for trade test.

Thursday, March 21st   There was an air raid last night, it is thought to be a Zepp. Some distance from here but they have got the "wind up". No lights after 7 p.m. whereas there have been strong lights before.

Good Friday, March 22nd   Anti-aircraft guns brought here, quite a lot of them on lorries. A lot of civilian natives going up the line to work on the land.

Saturday, March 23rd   Officer just told us that timber has reached £1 per cubic foot and it's rotten at that.

Monday, March 25th   Started a brick field on the job as they cannot keep me supplied. Several chaps sent here for a month's course, all bricklayers. Don't understand it, they know nothing of the trade.

It rained all night and best part of today but it will soon be finished.

> On March 25th General Allenby was ordered to send troops to France because of the German offensive on March 21st where they swept across the British positions on both sides of the Somme.
>
> Indian troops were planned for Palestine before the German offensive to replace British battalions of the 10th, 60th and 75th Divisions with no intention of sending troops to France.
>
> From March 21st to April 21st casualties in France amounted to 225,000. There were 30,000 reinforcements in France with 180,000 drafts at home. For the next 3–4 months Britain could only find 23,000 men per month − mostly from Reserves.
>
> *History of the Great War*

Friday, March 29th   It has been a very bad one for us out on the sand. A strong south wind came on very hot and choking then there was a sand storm. It was awful. We laid in a little hut with eyes shut. Nearly choked with fine sand that came through the cracks in the boarding. Then came the rain which lasted for some hours.

A rare lot of men still coming for trade test.

Saturday, March 30th   Had a whist drive in the mess hut. Quite a nice change. About one hundred sat to play.

Monday, April 1st   Summer time started − drill clothes issued.

Tuesday, April 2nd   Seven men were transferred from the 570th to Ludd to join a new water company. Among them was Gardener who came from Pier Cellars with me. Issued with sun helmets.

Was lucky enough to draw a ticket for Miss Lena Ashwell's concert party at Y.M. So many wanted to get in besides the lucky ones that the doors and windows were burst in, chairs were smashed in the rush and crush inside. I quite expected to see the whole building collapse − and it is not exactly a castle − but all quietened down and the concert was fine.

> Lena Ashwell (1872−1957) was a leading London actress of the period. She organised entertainment for the troops in the form of concert parties after initial rejection by the Authorities. Concerts were free in the camps.
>
> *Myself a Player by L. Ashwell*

Friday, April 5th   52nd Division passing through here − on their way home? or France? Anyway, getting nearer after three years. Passed our camp, singing, all night long.

The 52nd Division were on their way to France.

History of the Great War

Saturday, April 6th   Have put sand bag revetment around tents as protection against air raids. Had none here yet.

Sunday, April 7th   Sapper Gardener returned to our Company. Bricklayers not wanted. Met five men of the Ceylon Police in Machine Gun Corps − they have been in the Kings Royal Rifles at Sheerness. They came from southern India and cannot speak to any of the other Indians here as they come from the north.

Thursday, April 11th   I am working close to the railroad which goes to the line. For days there have been troops, horses, guns, wagons etc. coming down. It makes one think the war is over. They say that our base is going down to Alexandria and that Colonial and Indian troops are going to finish it up here. I don't expect it will make any difference to us R.Es.

Infantry leaving Kantara.   *Institution of Royal Engineers*

Friday, April 12th   One year of service completed. Rather different weather from when I joined. It was snow and frost then, now it is scorching sun.

The Hindus are having a festival − it is a queer turn-out.

Saturday, April 13   Some of the 74th Division have come here on their way somewhere else. Met Goldsmith, a Ramsgate boatman, now a driver in the R.Es.

Hindus still on with their festival.

The 74th Division were on their way to France.

History of the Great War

Troop Train at Kantara.

Imperial War Museum

Friday, April 19th Bengal Lancers arrived here from France. British troops still coming down from the line, Indians going up.

> The official records give no mention of the Bengal Lancers being in Egypt or Palestine at this time but the following Cavalry units of the Indian Army were there during the period June 1917–18:—

2nd Lancers	6th Cavalry
9th Hodson Horse (4th Lancers)	18th Lancers
19th Lancers	20th Deccan Horse
29th Lancers	34th Poona Horse
36th Jacob's Horse (The Scindle Horse)	38th Central India Horse
1st Hyderabad Imperial Service Lancers	Jodhpore Imperial Service Lancers
Mysore Imperial Service Lancers.	

> *History of the Great War*

Indian Army Cavalry at Kantara.   *Institution of Royal Engineers*

Saturday, April 20th Cape Corps arrived from German East Africa. Nearly all speak English. Three companies of R.Es. now at work on our job extending the Indian Base Depot.

> This was the 1st Cape Corps from South Africa − a native battalion part of the 53rd Division.
> *History of the Great War*

Monday, April 22nd Now have 200 Egyptians and 300 Indians to look after on the works. All the help I have is a corporal at times − tired out every day but it won't last forever. It is very hot now.

Tuesday, April 23rd We have had a severe sandstorm. We got the full benefit being out in the desert. Work was stopped as it was impossible to open one's eyes. The sand blew so fiercely that it cut face and legs. Lasted all day. I would rather have rain for it was hot and hard to breathe. Timber, nails and all sorts of things will have to be dug out.

Sunday, April 28th   Had a pass so spent a nice quiet day at Ismailia in the Wilderness Gardens. Saw the statues of the ancient Kings of Egypt. Very crude but carved out of one block of red granite. Quite a group of them there.

The 70th Division gone through. A lot of Ramsgate chaps with them in the 10th East Kent Rifles. Met Corporal Emptage, R.A.M.C. (Sanitary Section) of Margate who tells be Thorncroft of Ramsgate is here.

Monday, April 29th   Spent the evening with young Thorncroft, the baker's son of Dumpton Park Drive, Ramsgate. It was a treat to see someone who came from the same place. He said he had a lot to see him last week and mentioned names. I knew all of them. Thorncroft is in the R.A.M.C. (S.S.) duty at Kantara East station so he sees a lot he knows.

Tuesday, April 30th   Met "Togs" Price of Ramsgate, son of Mrs. Mumford bathing proprietor. He was just off to France.

Thursday, May 2nd   Cape Corps started working for us, getting a mixture now. They are dark skinned but all speak English.

Friday May 10th   Concert for all under the Assistant Director of Works by Miss Lena Ashwell's Concert Party.

> The concert party was made up of soprano, contralto, instrumentalist, tenor, baritone or base, entertainer and accompanist. All were professionals and some 600 artists were involved throughout the War period.
>
> *Myself a Player L. Ashwell*

Saturday, May 18th   Left the Company camp and have built a hut in the desert close to our work at the Indian Base Depot − a corporal and two sappers. We have our food with the British Personnel Indian Army in the Sergeants' Mess. We prefer to live on our own, so cook for ourselves. We have brought our own and had fried steak and onions. The best dinner I've had in the army. Plenty of tea. Have made bedsteads, using sailcloth for springs. Quite a treat. Out in the desert and nobody to trouble us, not another hut or tent within a mile of us.

Wednesday, May 29th   Funeral of Corporal Lang, Kantara cemetery. He died of fever. A married man with three children. Only had four days.

> The Regimental War diary states that Corporal Lang died of typhus fever at 4 a.m. and was buried at 2.30 p.m. the same day.
>
> *Institution of Royal Engineers Library*

Friday, May 31st   A terrible day − a south wind blowing across the desert. It is just like a baker's oven opening. We can't stand it. Obliged to be in a hut nearly all day. The worst we have experienced so far. It finished up with a sandstorm in the evening. Hope we don't get many days like that.

Sunday, June 9th   An Indian Military Band came this afternoon to play to the patients. They were from the Outram Regiment. They played English music. It was a treat to hear "Twilight", "Girl in the Taxi", "Mother Macree" etc. I quite enjoyed it.

Sunday, June 16th   Troops of the 60th and 10th Divisions are passing through on their way to France.

Tuesday, June 18th   A pest of mosquitoes has started. I am bitten all over. Some have turned bad but can get them dressed at this hospital. Neck and arms very bad. Have now got mosquito net, glad of it too.

Wednesday, June 19th Three thousand Artillery arrived here from Mesopotamia on their way to France.

An 18 pounder Q.F. Gun with sand pads (also used in mud). *Institution of Royal Engineers*

Friday, June 21st Only 198 Turkish prisoners of war reported to us for work out of 350 – all the rest gone sick. Some of those are not able to work, they die off like flies. About 12,000 here and 400 died last month and there will be more than that this month. They are drinking water all day long and care not where it comes from. The Egyptians can drink the Sweet Water without harm but it is death to us and it is the same with the Turks. They have a lot of Armenian doctors to attend to them. There will be trouble about it.

> Many Turkish prisoners were in a deplorable condition of health owing to a prolonged shortage of food. They suffered mostly from Malaria, Influenza, Pallagra (an obscure disease, caused by the absence of vitamin B) and ophthalmia, severe inflammation of the eye, which caused Napoleons troops in Egypt and Palestine so much trouble.
>
> *A Brief Record of the Advance of the E.E.F 1917–1918   Tabers Cyclopedic Medical Dictionary*

Thursday, June 27th Met Stanley Lane, R.Q.M.S. 2nd/24th Londons who is in a camp only three minutes' walk from our works at the Indian Base Depot. They have been there a month and I didn't know it.

I received a notice from the Assistant Director of Works respecting a nuisance. It was signed by lieutenant-colonel commanding 2nd/24th Londons. I soon went across and found Stan and had a long chat; he was just as much surprised as I. They expect to go to France soon.

Friday, June 28th In the evening went to see Stan and the 2nd/24th concert party. It made quite a change.

Anzac Engineers erecting stables at Kantara.

Institution of Royal Engineers

Friday, July 5th Met Jack Isaacs of Ramsgate who expects to go back to the front in the Northamptons.

Sunday, July 7th Proceeded to Cairo for seven days' leave. Have put up at a very fine hotel, the Eden Palace facing Esbekeik Gardens. A good bed with mosquito net and proper bedroom furniture. Dining room and lounge are very nice. Plenty of palms so pleasant to the eyes after so much sand. We went to Luna Park at Heliopolis, a White City on a small scale, and listened to a band in the Esbekeik Gardens in the evening.

Monday, July 8th Had a good look round and a rest in the gardens. Good food and then a sleep on the grass which was a holiday in itself after so much sand.

Tuesday, July 9th Hired a guide at 30 Pts. a day, the same one Lord Brassay and Lord Haldane had. He showed us their recommendations. Had a garry and went round the tombs of the Mamelukes and the Imperial Family. They are handsome things. Lovely carving on the tomb of Ibrahim Pasha, the man who fought against us at Tel-el-Kebir. It cost £24,000 but would cost ten times that in England. Then to the Citadel and the lovely mosque built therein of alabaster stone where all the Mamelukes were killed. It is the finest building I have ever seen. Then to the mosque built of stone taken off the outside of the Great Pyramid.

In the afternoon we went to Giza, about a nine-mile tram ride through an avenue of lovely trees and over the Nile. At the end of the tramway we took donkeys to ride up a great hill round the Pyramids, Sphinx, Temple and the tombs excavated by the English where the mummies came from that are in the British Museum.

Back to Cairo and the theatre in the evening.

Here the author appears to have mis-recorded the original. Ibrahim Pasha was commander of the Egyptian forces in Greece from 1825 to 1827 and therefore opposed the British, French and Russian fleets at Navarino on 20 October 1827, the last great battle fought between sailing ships. The commander of the Egyptian forces opposed to Sir Garnet Wolseley's army at Tel-el-Kebir on 13 September 1882 was Arabi Pasha.

R. J. Crampton

Wednesday, July 10th We went to the Zoological Gardens, a very nice place with plenty of trees, plants and animals. Then to El-Roda Island. We saw Pharaoh's Palace and the place where Moses was found in the bullrushes. Next, the Old Gate of Babylon, then to the old Coptic Church and saw the spot where Mary and Christ rested when first arriving into Egypt, also the spot where Joseph rested. This was in a vault under the old church. Then on to the first mosque built in Cairo − 365 columns in it. The column that flew from Mecca, the healing stones where they rubbed lemon and licked it and then went away healed, and the good and bad man columns. An old doorway with the original paint still good.

Pictures in the evening.

Thursday, July 11 Started for the Barrage of the Nile. First a long tram ride then two hours on a steamboat down the Nile, a very wide river. Millions of water melons growing on the banks. At the Barrage there are lovely gardens. The guide brought roast chicken meat, bread, cheese, butter, pickles and a large melon. We had quite a picnic under the trees. He then took us on a trolley pushed by two natives and explained the working of the Barrage which sends water from the Nile to various parts of Egypt, then on the boat again and back to the hotel having spent a nice day near the river.

Barrage of the Nile.

Institution of Royal Engineers

Friday, July 12th Spent a day looking round Cairo and having a good rest.

Saturday, July 13th A trip to the Museum to see the old jewels, mummies and statues of Ancient Egypt. After that we went though the native and European bazaars – very interesting.

Had a good feed and caught the train back to Kantara feeling much better for the change but sorry to go back again.

Monday, July 15th One Turkish prisoner attacked the Indian sentry and was killed. The sentry fired four rounds at him on our brickfield.

Saturday, August 17th WE SHALL WIN! We have just had orders never to salute an officer with the left hand again. Now just fancy nobody thinking of that before! What a lot of strife it may have saved. To make doubly sure of winning we must now always put putties on and button up our coats when going outside the camp. We are in the desert sixteen miles from the nearest village and not more than twenty civilians within that distance. The staff of the British Army are waking up?

I think we have got over the hottest part of the summer, it was 104° to 110° in the shade for some weeks and we had to start work at 6 a.m. Breakfast before we started work, until 12 noon, then we had a pint of tea and two small slices of bread and marmalade. Started work again at 2 p.m. until 5 p.m. then they wondered why so many men went to hospital. The last few days have been a treat, only 90° in the shade. Fancy feeling cool in a temperature of 90° in the shade. What shall we do when the winter comes?

Wednesday, August 28th Indian Base and Hospitals almost finished so I have gone to build red brick wall around the European Cemetary, British and Turkish soldiers mostly.

Thursday, August 29th Today two sappers of the Kent Fortress R.Es came to me for trade test. The superior one of them belongs to Sittingbourne, the other, Sapper F. Chandler of Broadstairs I know well as he was apprenticed to Jack May. He also used to attend the class of Building Construction at Ramsgate Secondary School under Whitehead of Margate. Returned to Company at South Bridge Camp by the Canal.

Sapper "Son" Chandler served with the 111 Kent Field Royal Engineers and was one of the few survivors of Gallipoli. He then served under General Allenby in Palestine and was demobbed from the Crystal Palace in the summer of 1919. He died at the age of 67.

Monday, September 2nd Have started building Court Martial room and shelter.

Friday, September 13th Two large transports have just discharged troops at the wharfs built by us in the Suez Canal. These are the first troops landed here.

Saturday, September 14th Building wire fence around Sisters' quarters at 44th Hospital.

Friday, September 20th Reported sick with fluid on left knee. Two months ago the right knee was treated at the Indian Hospital for same trouble but soon got better, thanks to a kindly captain and staff-sergeant who attended to my leg three times a day for ten days. Today I arrived at reception tent 7 a.m., saw doctor 7.45, result housemaid's knee. Massage, iodine and bandage, one day light duty. Waited one hour at dressing tent No. 1 then sent to No. 2. Was attended to at 10.45. Arrived back in camp and C.S.M. told me to rest in my tent all day.

A lot of wounded brought down from the line today, also Turkish prisoners. Heavy fighting.

Sapper F. Chandler.

Saturday, September 21st Reported sick – four days' massage with iodine and bandage *and* duty as usual but I am taking it easy. I can't get about very well. Half the company are working all night building compounds for prisoners just taken.

Sunday, September 22nd Nearly all the company working on compounds. 3,000 prisoners arrived this morning and over 20,000 expected so we are busy. I still have the same job but can't get about fast enough – good job too.

Monday, September 23rd Another 4,000 Turkish prisoners arrived here today making us very busy. Rations will be cut down again I expect.

Thursday, September 26th Anniversary of leaving England today. We are given two blue chevrons for service abroad. I hope to be home before getting the third. It has been a sight this last few days – German, Austrian and Turkish prisoners have come here in thousands in a deplorable condition. Germans are in the best condition. We are all building cages for them so busy day and night. I am working at Headquarters today putting down Ballat floors.

Kantara – Egyption Labour Corps and Turkish prisoners unloading at the Quay.

Imperial War Museum

Tuesday, October 1st   What a rain storm! The first rain since March and we knew it, it flooded all around every tent. Had from four to twelve inches in them − everything soaked.

Wednesday, October 2nd   Reported sick with knee which is no better. Three days' medicine and dressing, duty as usual.

Thursday, October 8th   Started building prison cells for P.o.W in compounds. I hope they stop taking Turks, they feed them at our expense. Rations are awful now, although a lot of stuff lies at the dump going rotten.

I have finished going to hospital. I am tired of their treatment and they have done no good to the knee. Have not been able to draw pay although pay book shows £8.8.0. credit. Chatham pay office has brought me into debt, I don't know what for, have asked for a statement of accounts. In the meantime, no pay no work.

Friday, October 11th   I am now receiving treatment for my knee at the Turkish hospital; I have to go there to do jobs. It is improving now.

Monday, October 14th   Strong rumours of Germany accepting Allies' terms − nothing official.

Tuesday, October 15th   Filled in form giving wife power to vote for me at General Election.

Thursday, October 17th   Paving lawn tennis court − mud brick on edge, herring-bone bond and plastered with clay.

German Artillery officers surrendering at Amman.   *Institution of Royal Engineers*

Sunday, October 20th   Funeral of Sapper Kerswell at Kantara Cemetery.

Monday, October 21st   One year completed in Kantara. We started shorter working hours today, 7 a.m. till 12.0, 1.30 p.m. till 4.30 p.m.

The meat ration has been cut down so as to have extra bacon for brecky. We find the bacon rotten, that is why they want to get rid of it. There are tons of cheese going rotten up at the Main Supply Depot. We shall get that soon when it is quite bad. The bread we get now is filthy. It is nearly time the war finished.

Thursday, October 24th   Jack Isaacs called to see me. We had a sandstorm. At first it looked like smoke from a fire, then it spread all over the sky. A little later we caught it, could not see a yard in front of you, it lasted about an hour after thunder and lightning.

Friday, October 25th   Heavy rain storm. The place all flooded up at the Infantry Base. There are hundreds of men just returned from the hospital. No tents, no place to get under. All lying on the sand wet through yet P.o.Ws are in new tents eight to each. Tommy is of no account.

Troops are again leaving this country, yet strange today two big ships have brought more troops here from Blighty.

My knee is a bit better, now I have got a touch of the sun. Violent pains in the head for a week now and still in the sun for eight hours a day.

Sunday, October 26th   Had a lively afternoon − the labourers had a fight with the masons. Trowels, shovels, rammers were all used. I managed to stop it after knocking a few down with a big stick. I sent several to Egyptian hospital badly hurt, luckily they did not turn on me. They are afraid of us. It's a good job too as I was alone with thirty of them. I had to report the lot, shall hear more of it.

Wednesday, October 30th   53rd Division going away, also a lot of R.A.F. Jack Isaacs leaving Kantara escorting P.o.Ws. R.E. theatre opened with the Vagabonds party. The Royal Field Artillery loading stores ship in the Canal.

Thursday, October 31st   We have been told that hostilities cease on this front at 12 noon. The Turkish P.o.Ws were told I think as there was a lot of cheering in their camps. The Egyptian Labour Corps also cheered but British are too fed up to cheer and very little was said about it.

Friday, November 1st   Winter rations start. Cheese for midday meal − the first piece since March 30th.

Monday, November 4th   News posted up at General Headquarters of the armistice with Austria − no excitement at all.

Wednesday, November 6th   Sergeant Simmonds taken to hospital, collided with a push trolley on the railway whilst riding motor bike.

A lovely smell of boiling bacon prevails in Kantara. About 150 tons of bacon have gone bad so being used at the By-Products factory for soap etc.

Monday, November 11th   AT LAST CESSATION OF HOSTILITIES. How we waited for the news to come through! We heard it was alright and at 8.10 p.m. an officer came to the canteen and told us the news. Up in the Indian Base Depot rockets were sent up and also from the monitor lying in the canal. Everyone merry and bright but we are still in the army, as we got in trouble for having our candle alight at 9.45 p.m. when it should have been put out at 9.30.

Last night a party from the Indian Base Depot raided the officers' mess. Shared out the drink and took the piano out to the roadway and had a singsong. Then they carried it about

1½ miles to the English military prison and gave a concert outside − they got into trouble for that.

The last of the 53rd passed through here this morning.

Tuesday, November 12th   Flags are up at the Suez signal station and a big boat came through with all its flags flying. My Gippos had never seen anything like that in their lives and went mad over it.

Friday, November 15th   Orders issued from G.H.Q. telling officers and N.C.Os to use *tact* in dealing with men. "Give them sports and make duties as light as possible." There has been trouble here between officers and men and I may say the officers were afraid to deal with them. Officers who have been bullies have had a rough time of it.

A Monitor.

Saturday, November 16th   A smoking concert arranged for tonight. Band to attend. A 2½ Pt. ticket given to each man.

Sunday, November 17th   A whole day off, no parade at all. The easiest day I've had in the Army. 569th Army Troop Company, Devon, arrived in Kantara. I went to the Remount Depot to dinner and spent the evening there.

Monday, November 18th   Back to Indian Base to work − helmets withdrawn.

Thursday, November 21st   Started building camp for returned P.o.Ws − 200 Gippos and 300 Indians, one company Queen Victoria's Lehore and Madras. All rush.

Saturday, November 23rd   After working at top speed with 600 men I now have to pull the camp down and clear it all away! Then they say "don't lose interest in your work".

A remount camp with special lines for sick horses at Deir-el-Belah.

Institution of Royal Engineers

Monday, November 25th   Met Thorncroft again − on duty at Kantara East station. Had a lecture about demobilization, many questions were asked. The terms are likely to cause trouble.

Wednesday, November 27th   Another lecture upon demobilization. One corporal asked if, when peace was settled whether we should have to work nine hours a day in the sun, or work under peacetime conditions? Refused an answer.

Friday, November 29th   I met Will Long of the 10th Middlesex (Lily Ryan's husband) in the Y.M.C.A. He is now in the Essex Regiment and had just come out of hospital.

Saturday, November 30th   Our own concert party gave a turn in the R.E. theatre. The first in public, they were very good. General Lloyd was present with staff. Will Long came with me. They are called "The Decauvilles" after the light railways used by R.Es.

Egypt	Killed and died of wounds		Died of sickness and other causes		Total deaths	
	Officers	Other ranks	Officers	Other ranks	Officers	Other ranks
Regimental and Territorial forces	729	8231	247	5371	976	13602
Colonials	109	1295	34	762	143	2057
Indians	57	1469	10	1877	67	3346
Totals	895	10995	291	8010	1186	19005

EGYPTIAN EXPEDITIONARY FORCE as at 30th November 1918:
14,230 Officers   300,170 Other ranks
1,177 Nurses   87,801 Egyptian Labour Corps

Statistics of the Military Effort of the British Empire during the Great War 1914–20   The War Office: March 1922. Published by H.M.S.O.

Wednesday, December 4th   All Turkish P.o.Ws are being withdrawn from works. Work is getting slack here now and a good proportion of the company have gone to Ismailia to work. I am to remain here worst luck. It has been a sight lately to see troops and material come down from the line.

Have just noticed date stones growing, coming up like a nice palm.

Saturday, December 7th   Repairing and decorating buildings which are to be headquarters for the 75th Division who are to garrison Kantara. Jack Isaacs came down. His regiment is going down close to Cairo tomorrow. Heaps of transport and troops still going down that way.

Sunday, December 8th   Had a pass to Ismailia but it was cancelled and I had to work as usual. I had to go to the Egyptian Labour Corps camp for labour and saw some of them undergoing punishments. Some were tied by the wrists to posts at a height so that they were unable to stand flat on the ground. Others were in "stocks", hands and feet locked and sitting on a board one inch thick. Others were lifting various sized stones off the ground to arms' length above their head.

Lieut. Col. (temp. Brig-Gen) A. H. O. LLOYD, C.B., C.M.G., M.V.O. Commander Canal zone, Palestine lines of communication.   Institution of Royal Engineers

49

Monday, December 9th   Received Christmas parcel from home. Everything good. The Mummers Concert Party gave a turn in our theatre.

Major-General Patin, 75th Division, has taken his quarters here.

Tuesday, December 10th   Saw Jack Isaacs of Northants on his way to Cairo concentration camp.

No tobacco ration for three weeks. I suppose they look upon it as peace time, but when it touches work we are still on active service.

Friday, December 13th   Had pass to Ismailia but it was cancelled owing to disturbances among the soldiers and police so went to Port Said. Tons of shipping in the harbour. One pint bottle of Bass is 2/8d. Tobacco is 9 Pt. for 4 oz. Two boxes of matches for 1 Pt.

An early French iron clad battle ship of about 1890 at Port Said. 1918.   Institution of Royal Engineers

Tuesday, December 17th   A general holiday for the troops here. All we had to do was a church parade at which every unit was represented. It was in a big theatre that was built out of canteen funds six months ago and never used.

Wednesday, December 18th   I am now working at the 44th Stationary Hospital and it is awful to see the poor fellows taken out under the flag; six or seven every day, mostly 'flu cases and to be kept under canvas at this time of year it is serious for them. While this is happening all the H.Q. staff and staff of the 75th Division occupy the only brick buildings there are in the district. They ought to be thrown out of it, it's disgusting. The hospital staff do all they possibly can but it's the tents that do the damage.

Plenty of Jaffa oranges to be got now, three big ones for 1 Pt. – about 2½ d.

It is said that Spanish Flu, as it became known, killed more people than the war.

Saturday, December 21st   Most of the Egyptian Labour Corps have gone home and they are replacing them with infantry of the 75th Division, repairing roads, unloading boats etc. – this is the reward for four years' hard fighting. In many cases they have refused to work. Yesterday a large party was brought to the canal from their camp six kilometres distant, then set to unload a big ship. They refused. General Lloyd was sent for but they still refused so were sent back to camp – they claim it is not a country for white men to work hard and they are quite right. Having fought out here as they have they ought to be given plenty of time off now. Trouble is brewing all around. Officers are having a fine time and men still hard at work. All ammunition, fuses and explosives have been withdrawn from the company.

Sunday, December 22nd   Have today filled in the civil employment form.

Monday, December 23rd   Started building camp for 21st Corps of Tractor companies at Kilo 7, Ducidar Road. The caterpillars have arrived. Had to pull down all the work done today and rebuild it on the opposite side. Had a little rain today.

Tuesday, December 24th   Still busy among the caterpillars. About sixty natives to look after.

Picked up an Egyptian fob chain today. It was in a little ant hill that I kicked over. Received letter from Jessie with Christmas greetings. It was given to me at 6 p.m. also bundle of papers.

Holt (American) Caterpillar Tractors drawing abandoned enemy material out of Beersheba.   Institution of Royal Engineers

Wednesday, December 25th – Christmas Day No work, no reveille, no parade, plenty of food so had a good time. It is quite hot in the sun so we don't want jackets on.

Breakfast 7.30 a.m. – porridge, bacon, bread and jam. Dinner 1 p.m. – turkey, green peas, potatoes, bacon, and beef stuffing, one bottle beer and plenty of Christmas pudding made in our own cookhouse. It was splendid. Tea 4.30 p.m. – bread and jam, mince pies and rock cakes. After 6 p.m. beer in the canteen. Lights out 10.15. All the troops appear to have had a good time so the trouble expected did not happen.

Saw Corporal Clayson of 1st/4th Buffs, also Griggs of King Street, Ramsgate, just arrived with 1st/5th Buffs from Mesopotamia.

Thursday, December 26th Work as usual. It is very hot today, walking about in shirt sleeves.
Have been offered £10 by Tewfik Affendi for the chain I found on Christmas Eve.

Friday, December 27th First one of the Company gone to General Base Depot for demobilization. Sapper Till and all men of 41 years warned to be ready.
Built a ramp over pipe track for caterpillar tractors.

Fred standing on the left – 28 December 1918 Kantara.

Monday, December 30th No. 2 Indian Base Depot turned into transit camp for demobilization. About 5,000 men are there with no accommodation. Half have to sleep in the open and it is now very cold at night. Food is also very short and no place to cook.

Tuesday, December 31st The men who have been sent to the demobilization camp from this company have come down to get some food – they are almost starving up there.

1919

Wednesday, January 1st   Half day off work, sports in the afternoon. Very hot today. We had Christmas pudding for dinner and it was good.

Saturday, January 4th   Four more men gone to hospital with 'flu. Half the Company have colds, illness is very bad in demob. camp. About 10,000 there and only accommodation for 2,000. We are very busy making it better in every way. R.S.Ms, C.S.Ms, sappers, privates, all mixed up and fighting for their food.

Sunday, January 5th   First batch departed for Blighty; about 700 in the train for Port Said. They marched past here all merry and bright.

Monday, January 6th   About 500 more for Blighty.

Saturday, January 11th   A lot of our company in hospital seriously ill, they were not taken in until their cases were serious. They are now issuing oil cake for fuel by the ton, yet storing bad wood − a wicked shame.

Returning from work in a lorry Gunner Eldridge (who is attached to the R.E. and working with me) was sitting on the tail-board, the Gippos inside. We had fastened it up ourselves, he one side, I the other. After going a little way it gave out. I managed to cling tight but he went into the road. I got a hospital car to take him to the reception station where he lay on the stretcher for 1¼ hours before the M.O. saw him. By that time he had pulled round and was much better when I left him.

Sunday, January 12th   Sapper Bagwell buried, the whole company followed. He leaves behind a wife and six children all under ten years' old and his life was played with. He was sent back to camp medically discharged for ten days last Friday, January 10th. At 10.30 p.m. the Sgt. Major took him to hospital. He was placed on the danger list at once and died this morning at 2 a.m. No attention paid to him until he was dangerously ill. The company is up in arms about it and demand the Captain to enquire about it as this is the fourth case where death has taken place after being on medical discharge.

Tuesday, January 14th   About 4,000 left for Blighty today.

Enquiry about the gunner falling out of the lorry. I made a report against the M.O. being so long before he attended to him. I don't suppose it will go far though.

A big fire in the Ordnance dump but did not get called out.

Friday, January 17th   1,700 men started for Blighty, among them was Sapper Dunn, second man from this company.

Bacon is still being run down for soap, we have had no issue lately.

Tuesday, January 21st   Sapper H. Wallis has gone to General Base Depot − going home on compassionate leave. I met him at Chatham and we have been together all through. About 3,000 men went home yesterday and today.

Returned to 44th Hospital to work.

Thursday, January 23rd   Six men left the company for demob. camp. They are all men over 41 years. All detached men called back to the company.

Meeting called by O.C. to find out the reasons why men are not joining the new army. For 1½ hours he listened to various complaints we had. As he had given us freedom of speech he had to agree with most.

Saturday, January 25th   Sapper H. Wallis left Kantara for Blighty on compassionate leave.

Sunday, January 26th   Had the day at Ismailia. Saw P.C. Waters of Ramsgate at the Military Foot Police barracks. He left Ismailia for demob. camp Kantara. He is being sent home as he is over 41.

Monday, January 27th   Order issued by Major-General Wright, Chief Engineer, Egyptian Expeditionary Force, allows demobilizers and private men to go when called but no other man is to be released until further orders. There are many release-slip men in this company. All have been stopped − there will be trouble.

Tuesday, January 28th   Big *red* note placed upon the G.H.Q. notice board complaining about the way the departmental corps are being kept in this country and asking the men concerned to stop work and demand satisfaction. The corps complaining are the Army Service Corps, Royal Ordnance Depot, Royal Engineers, Army Ordnance Corps, Army Veterinary Corps. At night a meeting of protest as to the way we were being treated over demobilization was held, the O.C. being present. Some strong comments were made and the O.C. was asked to forward them to the Chief Engineer.

Saturday, February 1st   Issued with one pair of pants and one vest for wear in Haifa. Shall have to lie in bed whilst someone washes them for us having no change. "Slip" from Advisory committee arrived, cancelled.

Sunday, February 2nd   Detachment of 569 Coy., R.E. arrived to take over our camp and work.

A Crossley 23/30 Hp type truck. 4½ litre 5 bearing cylinder side valve engine. A tender for the Royal Flying Corps.   Institution of Royal Engineers

The Royal Naval Air service and the Royal Flying Corps merged on 1 April 1918 to become the RAF.

A RAF type Leyland 32Hp modified to 36hp possibly the most successful and satisfactory British Wartime Truck – some 6000 were built from 1914–1919.

Institution of Royal Engineers

Tuesday, February 4th   We left Kantara East at 12.45 p.m. with all our tool carts, wagons and horses. We were in trucks. *One* truck with sailcloth all over the roof and sides for three officers and their baggage; we were put thirty men *and* baggage in trucks of same size with no sides or roof. Scarcely room to sit down. We went across the desert then up along the coast. All the way was rough and hills spotted with native villages.

Wednesday, February, 5th   Arrived at Haifa 11.00 a.m. unloaded train. Our luck was in, there were lorries there to take our kit bags. They also took our equipment. We had to go to Mount Carmel which is about two miles from Haifa and about 900 ft. above sea level. It was about the most dangerous ride I've had in a motor. If anything had broken we should have run back and over the other side.

We look down upon Haifa, then the Bay and Acre on the other side. We are billetted in a big house built of stone with a tiled roof, about twelve men to a room. It is quite comfortable. They have a lot of rain here. Last night the wind howled outside. It was quite a strange sound with the rustle of trees. This is a rocky mountain but plenty of trees, grass and flowers all round. It is a change from the sand. We trample flowers under our feet that are sold by florists at home at a good price. Big Jaffa oranges six for 1 Pt. Tons of them here.

Thursday, February 6th   No work today, all fatigues – building cookhouse and rigging ourselves up in general. Nearest drinking water two miles away so eat oranges instead of drinking. No canteen or Y.M.C.A. The house we are in has been used by Germans as a hospital so has a Red Cross on the roof. Our windows look over the hills to the Mediterranean – very nice.

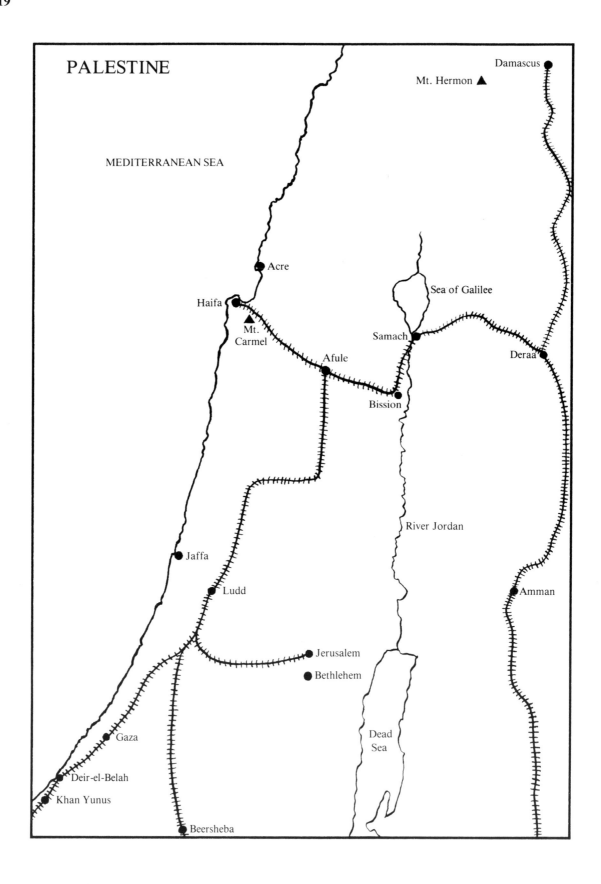

PALESTINE

MEDITERRANEAN SEA

Damascus

Mt. Hermon ▲

Acre

Haifa

Sea of Galilee

Mt.
Carmel

Samach

Afule

Deraa

Bission

River Jordan

Jaffa

Ludd

Amman

Jerusalem

Bethlehem

Dead
Sea

Gaza

Deir-el-Belah

Khan Yunus

Beersheba

Friday, February 7th Started work levelling sites for huts to accommodate the garrison. Strong wind and rain like Blighty.

Saturday, February 8th Sunday, no work. Had some lovely walks over the hills and down the Wadi. Looking to the north-west there are mountains with snow on the peaks. The high one is Mount Hermon. All sorts of flowers, plenty of birds singing. It is also nice to see and hear bees. None of that sort of thing at Kantara. There are also tortoises and plenty of scorpions under every bit of rock you shift.

A lot of Turks here. The natives are mostly Bedouins and Jews, the Bedouins have clothes of all colours with beads round their necks and tons of tassels on the donkeys' saddles too.

Lovely butter is to be had here 3/- lb. I had some, the first I have tasted since July 13th — it was a treat. Eggs are five for 1/- but are like Blighty ones.

Tuesday, February 11th Have been round looking at the German defence works. They must have left here in a hurry for there are two new 6″ guns made by Krupp in 1898. One is overlooking Haifa, Acre and the Bay — that is on the mounting completed. The other lies on the ground — the mounting only half done — no breech blocks and both ends plugged with wood as they left ordnance. Close by is a statue (or was) to Kaiser Wilhelm erected April 25th 1910. It was defaced and blown up. These guns and statue are in front of the house which General Allenby is going to occupy.

Wednesday, February 12th Have had the morning off work. A gale was blowing and we were unable to stand. It also blew away several huts we had erected. Had a gang of masons from Jerusalem and Beirut dressed like Bedouins.

Saturday, February 15th Heavy gale blowing the huts down again. Left off work at 2 p.m. — sent the Gippos home early to put up their tents before dark.

Tuesday, February 18th The O.C. explained the new method of demob. Also read out the names of men who are entitled to go, about forty-five go this week. 570th Company station, Haifa — 571st Company, Beirut.

Saturday, February 22nd Started alteration to drainage at General Allenby's house. It's a nice big house, but stairs and steps in all directions. All stone floors with cork lino stuck down. Lovely view of Haifa, the Bay and Acre on one side.

Sunday, February 23rd Twenty N.C.O's and men left this morning for demob. camp, Kantara — 1914 men, mostly between 22 and 25 years of age. There are still men of 39 and 41 years unable to get away although they joined in 1915.

Tuesday, February 25th Another draft of 1914 men gone to demob. camp, twenty-two N.C.O's and men, all senior N.C.O's gone. We are left with three corporals and three lance-corporals, Lieutenant Wibberly returned. He went to demob. camp two days ago but not being 51 years he was not able to go home yet.

Sunday, March 2nd Issued with vest, pants and leather jerkin.

Tuesday, March 4th Wind, rain, hail. Very cold. Notified that R.Es are entitled to 10/6d per week from February 1st.

Friday, March 14th Five men left for demob. camp, Kantara, four with over three and a half years' active service.

Wednesday, March 19th Four N.C.Os and fifteen sappers paraded before the O.C. We were told we had been promoted to various ranks, I to Corporal. We had no say in the matter. We were marched in and out of the orderly room just like defaulters.

Thursday, March 20th   I paraded with two other men before the O.C. and asked to revert to sappers. I think he will allow it now we are expecting to go home − if we took stripes we should have trouble to get away for a long time. One man over 41 years gone to demob.

Friday, March 21st   There is trouble now between the Jews and Arabs. Egyptian Labour Corps are also dissatisfied − several riots have occurred.

Promotions put in order but a line put through mine. It was dated 26th February 1919 so have been a corporal twenty-three days.

Saturday, March 22nd   Shifted from the billet into huts we have built.

Thursday, March 27th   Sharp firing was heard coming from Haifa − it lasted ten minutes, this is the third time. The trouble is one class of natives against the other.

Sunday, March 30th   Eight men left for demob. camp, Kantara.

Friday, April 4th   Shifted to huts half way down to Haifa.

Monday, April 7th   There are plenty of mosquitoes at night and flies by day. Mosquito nets issued to every man − now we have a little comfort.

Thursday, April 10th   Got five days' leave to Jerusalem. Started from Haifa at 11 a.m. in open trucks. Arrived Ludd 6.10 p.m. − slept on forms in the marquee at Y.M.C.A. Train for Jerusalem in the morning.

Friday, April 11th   Train left at 8 a.m. It is a perfect scenic railway. It takes a zigzag course through the valley. It is a marvel how they keep on the rails. The hills are all round and we went up hill all the way arriving at Jerusalem 10.50 a.m. A lorry met us at station and took us to a billet where we had good food and slept on stretchers.

In the afternoon we took a garry and went to Bethlehem − it is about one hour from Jerusalem. Saw Rachel's tomb then the Church of the Nativity, the birthplace of Christ. Went up to the top of the Russian tower to look over the shepherds' fields and Bethany. They are a very busy lot here working with mother-of-pearl, olive wood and stone from the Dead Sea.

Saturday, April 12th   Went with Y.M.C.A. guide into the Holy City − we entered by the Damascus Gate. Oh what a place! Half of it is under ground. All stone streets, almost impossible to walk as it is so slippery. We went to all the churches and places of interest. We passed the Last Stages of the Cross one by one up to the Church of the Holy Sepulchre. In this Church are the ornaments.

In the afternoon we went to the Mount of Olives. There is a fine church attached to the German Hospice. Worked in mosaic on the ceiling is the Kaiser and his wife holding up the church. We went up the tower, there was still a searchlight. From the top we had a fine view of the Dead Sea, River Jordan and valley. Then to the Russian Church and up that tower, the Church of the Lord's Prayer, Garden of Gethsemane, Tomb of the Virgin Mary and Solomon's quarries.

Sunday, April 13th   Had a look round outside the City, the lorry took us to the station and the train started at 1.30 p.m. for Ludd, a lovely trip. Went at a rapid pace down the hill for one hour ten minutes arrived Ludd 3.45 p.m. and spent the night in the Y.M.C.A. Just as we got to bed on the forms we were drowned with rain, everything soaked including blankets so we walked about all night to keep warm.

Monday, April 14th   Still raining. Started in open trucks for Haifa at 8.0 a.m. An awful journey. Gippo driver, bad engine and bad coal. Rain ceased, cold wind blowing. Arrived at Haifa 7.10 p.m., should have arrived at 1.30 p.m. Then had to walk up to camp. They issued rum to us and gave us dry blankets − glad of a night's rest.

Imperial War Museum

Demobilising Troops at Kantara.

Good Friday – April 18th   No work. A football match with Middlesex Yeomanry Army Service Corps. Heard that G.H.Q. are shifting to Cairo, that means all our work on Mount Carmel is useless. Rough estimate £800,000 – they have only just got there. No doubt officers (of which there are hundreds) find it too quiet and too far from Cairo.

Saturday, April 19th   Again offered promotion to take charge of detachment going to Damascus. Refused it with thanks.

Sunday, April 20th   Drew drill and helmet.

Monday, April 21st   Started from Haifa at 11.0 a.m. in carriage on the Turkish narrow gauge rail. At 12.10 we passed Afule – saw two antelopes there. Bission at 1 p.m. – hundreds of storks there. At 1.25 we passed over the bridge built by Canadian R.Es about 100 ft. above river bed. This place is 500 ft. below sea level, an awful place for fever. Two Bedouins put on train under armed escort, they had been placing obstacles on the line.

Reached Samach at 1.45 p.m. – there we ran along the Sea of Galilee into the valley of Samach. We soon came to a bridge with the engine pushing the train and another engine the other side. We were pushed on the bridge by one and pulled off by the other as the engines were too heavy to cross. Then we began the most wonderful railway I have seen in a zigzag course climbing up the hills. In one case we entered a tunnel at the bottom of the mountain, and came out at exactly the same spot but 800 ft. higher up. It was dangerous but a lovely sight to look down. It was like this for hours.

At last we got to the top and cleared the mountains at 5.30 p.m. There we saw an armed party carrying a red flag firing into a native village. We could see the dust fly up where the bullets hit. I didn't find out what the trouble was, they looked like Bedouins.

Sir Ross Smith, M.C., D.F.C., on the left – who flew the first Handley page aeroplane to India and was the first man to fly from Croydon, London, to Australia for which he was knighted.   *Institution of Royal Engineers.*

We reached Damascus at 11.30 p.m. and stopped the night in a tent by the station. Were woken up three times during the night by rifle shots.

Distance from Haifa to Damascus by rail 285 kilometres.

Tuesday, April 22nd   Telephoned to see where we were to report. An Indian cart was sent to take our kit but we had to walk three miles and were attached to the 21st (Indian) Sappers and Miners 9th Brigade. Stayed there all day, a very wild place.

Wednesday, April 23rd   Left the camp at 8 a.m. Two pack mules took our kit and we got to our destination at 11.20 a.m. about six miles south-west of Damascus.

Our job is to level the ground for an air station. This is one of the stages in the flight from England to India at the foot of Mount Hermon. There is snow on that all the year yet it nearly cooks a man at the bottom.

B Flight III squadron 1918.   *RAF Museum Hendon*

Sunday, April 27th   Day pass to Damascus − went there in an R.A.F. lorry. It is a very rough road, in many places the tram lines are simply laid on the road. Very narrow, dirty streets and miles of them roofed in with iron on circular arches. A lot had been taken by Germans for other use. Everybody seemed busy, the only place I have seen that. There is a brass factory in a rough wooden building just outside the city gate. Rare lot of youngsters who do the work that men would do at home, engraving and inlay work. It is all hand work, no machines and very expensive stuff.

We had revolvers lent to us by the R.A.F. No soldiers are allowed in the streets after dark − every night there is firing and very man is armed. They seem to shoot for the fun of it, mostly in the air but often at motor drivers because the cars frighten their camels which run for miles. The place is governed by the Hejaz men.

The R.A.F. is 'B' Flight 111 squadron.

> 111 Squadron was formed from 14 Squadron at Deir-el-Belah, Palestine, on August 1st, 1917 to support the army in Palestine and Syria as a fighter squadron. A variety of aircraft were used but were standardised on Niewports and SE5a's by 1918. They were equipped with Bristol fighters in February 1919.
>
> Their first victory was on October 8th, 1917 when 2nd Lieut. R. C. Steele, with Lieut. Lloyd-Williams as observer, shot down an Albatross Scout which was so little damaged that it was repaired and flown by 111 Squadron.
>
> By the end of the war "Treble-One" had destroyed 52 enemy aircraft.
>
> They became famous as the Black Arrows, the premier aerobatic team flying Hunters until 1961. They are now equipped with Phantom FGIs.
>
> *Fighter Squadrons of the R.A.F. and their aircraft*
> *III(F) squadron Fife Scotland*

Sunday, May 4th King Hejaz's son arrived home from France.

Monday, May 5th We went in a lorry to play football with the Middlesex Yeomanry, hardly able to get through the city. The streets and roofs crowded with people. Every man and most boys with pistols and swords all half mad, dancing, shouting and clashing swords. The streets all had arches built of trees with leaves on them. Coloured rugs and carpets covered the mud huts.

Halfway through we had to stop to allow the procession of King Hejaz's son and all this tribe to pass. The photo given in the Mirror of him is exact; we knew who it was at once. He is evidently thought a lot of here. There is no sign of British control − never a British flag to be seen − only Hejaz flags.

A Canadian called Fleming brought down the first German airman (Herr Dittmar in an Albatross Scout) at Deir-el-Belah. Fleming was flying a Bristol figher.

Institution of Royal Engineers

A Niewport 17 of III Squadron — A single fighting scout armed with one .303mm Lewis m/gun maximum speed at sea level 176km/h. *RAF Museum Hendon*

Bristol Fighters — maximum speed at 1000ft 111.5mph armed with .303 Vickers machine guns. *RAF Museum Hendon*

An unusual photograph of a SE5a of III squadron.
An SE5a single seat fighting scout, armed with one fixed .303 Vickers machine gun, one .303 Lewis machine gun on a mounting. Four 25 lbs Cooper Bombs. Span 27'11" speed at 10,000' 114 m.p.h.   *RAF Museum Hendon*

A BE2c nose down.

Institution of Royal Engineers

Tuesday, May 6th   Working at the Armenian camp and it wasn't too soon to get clear of it, not fit for an Englishman to be near. This is at Kaden Station.

Friday, May 9th   Left Kaden aerodrome and are stationed in the 21st Sappers and Miners camp.

Wednesday, May 21st   We left Sappers and Miners camp in a motor lorry. We got two days' rations and after a bit of a row we managed to take the Indian bivvy or we should have had to sleep in the open at the foot of the mountains. We are now ten miles south-west of Damascus close to Artux village. There are twenty-four farmers' families there in mud huts.

There are four of us with eight Indian guards. The nearest troops etc. are nine miles away. We are using water from a stream, our food is only half cooked as we have hardly any wood. This is the worst place for rations and general conditions I have had so far. We are to prepare a camp for Armenians who are leaving Kaden camp. It is so filthy they cannot live there any longer. They are the dirtiest and the laziest lot I have met. They are being kept by the Pioneers and Sappers, Royal Engineers, and some of them have more money than I ever had.

Tuesday, June 3rd   The Armenians will not stop here at Artux so the job has been washed out and we returned to the Sappers and Miners camp.

Wednesday, June 4th   The whole of the Sappers and Miners moved camp to a site one mile away, we with them.

Friday, June 6th   Reported sick about teeth — two extracted. The gums have left them and they are all loose. They can do nothing to stop them.

Friday, June 13th   One sapper arrived to replace another who is to return to company. This sapper is a 1916 man and has been a P.o.W. in Germany one year. Got back to England December 1st 1918, had two months' leave and was sent here after arriving May 21st.

Saturday, June 14th   Sapper James gone to Haifa.

Tuesday, June 24th   Heard of peace being signed at 8.30 p.m. Lights out as usual 9.30 p.m.

Thursday, June 26th   Left Damascus for Ludd 9.0 a.m., arrived Deraa 12.30. Departed 1.10 p.m., arrived Haifa 7.0 p.m. Spent the night at Y.M.C.A.

Friday, June 27th   Left Haifa 11.30 a.m. arrived Ludd 4.45 p.m. 20th Sappers and Miners three miles away so put up in the Y.M.C.A.

Saturday, June 28th   Telephoned to company for transport. Pack mule arrived 10.40 a.m., arrived camp 11.30 a.m. The C.S.M. soon had a double bell tent put up, each given a stretcher with two trestles for bed. He provided us with several good meals. So far it is a great improvement on Damascus.

At 8.0 p.m. news came through PEACE WAS SIGNED. Then the fun started, it was more like war than peace. Thousands of rounds were fired from rifles — numbers of bombs, bonfires, and fairy lights. Cheers and singing all round, only four English in our camp but the Indians soon got a bonfire and brought out their tom-toms. Instruments of all kinds but no players.

Monday, June 30th   General holiday but nowhere to go.

Monday, July 14th   General holiday owing to peace being celebrated throughout Egypt.

Sunday, July 20th   Day's pass to Jaffa, one hour train journey from Ludd. The railway is narrow gauge (decauville rail) with steam and motor engines. Jaffa is a fair sized place on the coast — quite a native town with small wharf for boats. Return fare 8 Pt.

Friday, July 25th   Returned to unit at Mount Carmel, Haifa. Only twelve men of the original company left. They now have Gippo cooks and things are not very clean. Eighteen months ago they were not allowed within a hundred yards of our cookhouses.

Monday, August 4th   Supposed holiday but work as usual for us.

Tuesday, August 5th   No native labour so we went back to our huts, sports in Haifa but unable to go there.

Friday, August 8th   Started job at soda water factory, Haifa. Billeted in town.

Saturday, August 9th   Another lot left for demob. Twenty-one men over 37 years of age and five for leave, having twenty-seven months' service in this country.

Wednesday, August 13th   Taken into 33rd Hospital sick. Nice clean place – on milk diet.

Monday, August 18th   Breakfast 5.0 a.m., moving down the line. Cancelled owing to a breakdown on the line.

Tuesday, August 19th   Left Haifa in fine Red Cross train at 7.45 a.m., arrived Ludd 10.30 a.m. Beef tea served out. Picked up another portion of Red Cross train after 110 kilometres. Departed Ludd 1.50 p.m. – Red Cross bag issued. Slept on train. Arrived Kantara 11.45 p.m. – almost deserted.

Wednesday, August 20th   Admitted to 24th Stationary Hospital 6 a.m.

Thursday, August 21st   Reported to dentist – three teeth taken out. Report again in ten days' time.

Friday, August 22nd   Four men in this ward who state they are quite fit for duty, refused to take seven injections. They were placed under arrest and guarded in a hut. The whole hospital resembles a prison.

Sunday, August 24th   The men who refused injections returned to ward under open arrest. One man who has taken them appears to be crippled in legs and unable to walk.

Tuesday, August 26th   Discharged from hospital.

Wednesday, August 27th   In R.E. details excused duty for seven days – to attend dispensary and dentist.
   Went to Kantara Theatre to see the comedy "The Naughty Wife". It was the best evening since leaving home – I was quite cheered up. Kantara is open to Egyptians now and they have built shops etc. Quite bright, but a deserted, military look about the place.

Tuesday, September 22nd   A draft of 700 men for demob. have been stopped to make room for Allenby and staff on boat.

Friday, September 5th   Slight rain during the night – first rain since April.

Saturday, September 6th   New teeth fitted – feel alright.

Thursday, September 18th   Two battalions infantry arrived by ship in Canal, in a very dirty condition. No R.Es – all reinforcements have been 1916 men, they have only been here a few months but are going back. We are still waiting for our turn.

Friday, September 19th   Temporarily attached 360th Company R.Es, Kantara.

Saturday, September 20th   On duty at the pontoon bridge across the Suez Canal at Kantara.

Imperial War Museum

Main Road at Kantara Base.

More troops arrived, but demob. is slow. A few 1916 men (first three months) gone but a lot still waiting in camp. Only Derby men entitled to go yet.

Friday, September 26th First big draft of 1916 men − 800 men gone today.

Sunday, September 28th Another draft of 800 gone to Port Said.

Friday, October 3rd Second three months' men gone to demob. camp − one out of my tent. He came out here in July which was his first time out of England. There are many cases like that. Tried again for leave but told I must go back to the company which may be any day. Tons of troops keep arriving but they are slow in sending men home.

A lot of troops from India have gone up the Canal lately.

Monday, October 6th Gave particulars in for demob. on age limit, 36 on April 30th 1919. They say I am not under them here. I went to R.E. details − they say they have nothing posted to do with me because I am for up the line.

Worked all night on bridge. Troops coming across, a few hundred R.Es − the first to come out − all elderly men. These have mostly taken on for twelve months. I have spoken to several over 60 years of age.

Tuesday, October 14th Large draft for demob. − second three months' men.

Wednesday, October 15th Returned to General Base Depot, R.E. details.

Friday, October 17th Left Kantara 7.15 p.m. for the company.

Saturday, October 18th Arrived Haifa 3.45 p.m. taken to company by lorry.

Sunday, October 19th Demob. particulars taken.

Monday, October 20th Carmel detachment to work at Soda Water Factory, the same job as I left when going to hospital.

Friday, October 24th Reinforcements arrived. Twenty men, twelve over 50 years old and four over 60 years signed on for one year.

Saturday, November 8th Nearly all the 1916 men gone to demob. My name has been verified at H.Q., now I have to wait for 1917 allotment to come through.

Saturday, November 29th WAR GRATUITY placed in pay book up to the time of closing in August which means we have 2/6d. per week reduction of pay since August 1st.

Tuesday, December 9th Twenty-eight more men arrived as reinforcements to the company but no one being sent away for demob.

Thursday, December 11th Returned to Headquarters, Mount Carmel for demob.

Friday, December 12th Medical inspection − making out of papers.

Saturday, December 13th Left Haifa 1.20 p.m. in open trucks. Have had a lot of rain but fine for a start.

Sunday, December 14th Arrived at Khan Yunus at 11.30 p.m. last night − stopped in a siding. Soaking wet through, all our kit washing about in the truck. We couldn't proceed as a train had a smash down the line. Our engine went back to Gaza for water and the line has been washed away between us so that cannot get back. Now 10.30 a.m. and still wet.

Another start made at 11.10 a.m. − now fine. Arrived at Kantara East 9.0 p.m. Spent the night in the mess huts.

Railway station bridge over the Canal at Kantara.   *Institution of Royal Engineers*

Anzac's crossing railway station bridge at Kantara.   *Institution of Royal Engineers*

(3 17 5) W6938—GD1389 5,000,000 10/18 HWV(P598)   Army Form Z. 18.

CERTIFICATE OF EMPLOYMENT DURING THE WAR.

(To be completed for, and handed to, each soldier).

A soldier is advised to send a copy rather than the original when corresponding with a prospective employer.

It is particularly important that an apprentice whose apprenticeship has been interrupted by Military Service should have recorded on this form any employment in a trade similar to his own on which he has been engaged during such Military Service.

Regtl. No. *263445*   Rank *Sapper.*

Surname *MILLS*
(block letters)

Christian Names in full *FREDRICK. THOMAS*

Regt. *R. E*   Unit *570 A.T. Coy.*

1. Regimental Employment.

Nature of.		Period.
General Construction From *20/10/17*	To *12/13/19*
(b)	"	"
(c)	"	"
(d)	"	"

*2. Trade or calling before Enlistment (as shown in A. B. 64).

Builders Foreman.

3. Courses of Instruction and Courses in Active Service Army Schools, and certificates, if any.

(a)

(b)

(c)

(d)

*The trade or calling must be filled in by the O.C. Unit from the Appendix to Special Army Order No. 6, of 21st October, 1918 (329 of November, 1918).

[P.T.O.

His certificate of employment during the war.

4. Military qualifications as shewn in A. B. 64.

---

5. Special Remarks as to qualifications, work done, or skill acquired during service with the Colours. This is required as a help in finding civil employment.

Very capable man at building work.

Soldier's Signature
(For identification purposes).   Signed _____ (Rank)

F. J. Mills   CAPT. R.E.

Commanding _____(DEVON) A.T. Co. (Unit)

NOTES.—The object of this certificate is to assist the soldier in obtaining employment on his return to civil life. The form will be completed as soon as possible in accordance with Demobilization Regulations.

As soon as signed and completed it will be given to the soldier concerned and will remain his property. He should receive it as early as is compatible with making the necessary references in order that he can either send it home or keep it in his possession.

One form will be issued to each man, and no duplicate can ever be issued.

The reverse side of certificate.

Monday, December 15th   Papers checked – all correct. Put in "E" section (Wimbledon or Shornecliffe). Camp crowded.

Tuesday, December 16th   Medical – kit and rifle inspection. Blankets disinfected and bath.

Wednesday, December 17th   Shifted into other tents but all are crowded. Eleven, twelve, thirteen and fourteen men to a tent. Also a fight to get food.

Thursday, December 18th   Fatigue cleaning camp.

Friday, December 19th   Fire picquet.

The Teutonic.   *National Maritime Museum*

The Teutonic *– built in 1889 by Harland and Wolff – was 9,984 tons and 568.8 ft. in length. Part of the White Star Line she sailed under a British Flag.*   *Lloyds Register*

Saturday, December 20th   Big draft picked for the *Teutonic* which sails on the 23rd regardless of when they came up for service. All 1916 men that are here and others who arrived in this camp up to December 12th. No arrivals now until after Christmas. About a hundred 1916 men arrived from the Sudan.

Sunday, December 21st   Officers' mess fatigue.

Monday, December 22nd   Little rain, sand storm – tents blown down. I get camp fatigues at night.

Tuesday, December 23rd   Sandstorm still on – all had to shift into other tents again. Some men of the draft missed a parade – a few struck off and others had one hour pack drill. Drafts for the *Teutonic* leave at 8 and 9 p.m.

CERTIFICATE

No. 263345 Rank *Sapper* Name *Mills F.*

Unit *570th (Devon) A. T. Coy.*

R. E.

Before your departure from the Egyptian Expeditionary Force and your re-entry into civil life, I wish to thank you for the valuable services you have rendered to the Army and the Nation.

Place *Mount Carmel* *W.Y BOWKER Lieut Col for* Brigadier General.

Date *13. 12. 19* Commanding *7th Infantry Brigade*

A.P.&S.D., Alex./6651/025c/63/3:19/75M. (V.&G.)

Certificate for service in Egyptian Expeditionary Force.

Wednesday, December 24th Another sandstorm, later rain. In tent all day. Rum issued.

Thursday, December 25th – Christmas Day Reveille 6 a.m., breakfast 7 a.m. Little butter, two eggs a man. Parade 8 a.m., warned for fire picquet. Had a fairly good dinner. Mounted picquet 3.30 p.m. A fine, warm day.

Friday, December 26th Warm, sunny day. Came off picquet at 4.0 p.m.

Saturday, December 27th Camp fatigue clearing drift sand in camp for five hours. Hundreds of men coming in, 600 in "E" section alone – some 1916 men.

Sunday, December 28th Church parade. The camp is overcrowded – a lot of men slept out last night. Have been busy all afternoon putting up tents. It is now a race and fight to get food which is awfully scarce. We have to buy practically all we want. More men arriving.

Monday, December 29th   Hundreds of men slept out last night − no tents for them. On fire picquet again.

Tuesday, December 30th   Came off picquet at 8.30 a.m. At 5.0 p.m. picked out for draft to sail on S.S. *Czar*.

> S.S. *Czar* − 6,516 tons and 319 feet in length − was built in 1912 by Barclay Curley & Co. of Glasgow; owned by the Russian East Asiatic Steam Co. Ltd., sailing under the Russian flag.
>
> *Lloyds Register 1919*

Wednesday, December 31st   Parade for draft. Roll call. Pay books taken. Medical inspection, exchange of money.

1920

Thursday, January 1st   Draft from "C" section left for hospital boat *Cordover* at 7.0 a.m. – Sapper Baker among them. Plenty of firing and shouting at midnight.

N.C.O's paid £1, others 10/- – dispersal papers taken. Paraded at 7.45 p.m., train left Kantara 11.15 p.m. – proper carriages.

Cordover – 4,933 tons – built by London and Glasgow Co. Ltd. in 1905 sailed under the Italian flag.

Lloyds Register 1919

Friday, January 2nd   Arrived Alexandria docks 8.0 a.m., boarded the S.S. *Czar* at 9.30 a.m. – seems to be a comfortable boat with fair amount of room for troops. I was lucky enough to get on top deck.

Left Alexandria at 4.30 p.m.

Saturday, January 3rd   Sea a bit rough.

Sunday, January 4th   Medical inspection.

Monday January 5th   Malta lights in sight 5.30 a.m., dropped anchor at 8.0 a.m. There are some good buildings here.

H.M.S. *Iron Duke* came in at 9.30 a.m., all lined up on deck and band playing. A lot of big boats came in, also two submarines. Discharged a little cargo and cleared the harbour at 2.0 p.m.

H.M.S. Iron Duke.   *Imperial War Museum*

At 4.15 p.m. we had boat drill. We were to have a concert on deck but the boat rolled so we could not stand − had it below. It was good. Plenty of plates and mugs, kitchen tackle rolling about the floor, very rough. Lay on the floor, could not sleep.

H.M.S. *Iron Duke* was laid down in June 1912 and completed in May 1914 by Laird at a cost of £1,891,122. Her normal displacement was:
Tonnage: 25,000
Length: 622′8″
Speed: 21 knots
Main guns: Ten 13.5″ Mark 5's
Compliment: 995−1022
Armour belt: maximum 12″
Other "Iron Duke class" Dreadnoughts were *Benbow, Emperor of India* and *Marlborough*.
H.M.S. *Iron Duke* was the flagship of Admiral Jellicoe while he was in command of the grand fleet. She took part in the Battle of Jutland on May 31st, 1916.

Janes Fighting Ships 1919

K15 − Though not in the Med. An interesting submarine of the period.   Imperial War Museum

A "K Class" submarine powered by steam turbine and diesel engine. Armed with one 4″ and one 3″ AA guns with eight 18″ torpedo tubes, 170 tons, 337′ long. Originally flush level bows showed a tendency to trim and dive on their own, so bows were raised.
Janes Fighting Ships

Tuesday, January 6th   Sighted land at 5.30 a.m. probably the African coast. At 10.0 a.m. we rounded a big rocky island which took hours. Coast in sight all day.

Wednesday, January 7th   Passed a lighthouse (or ship) at 6.0 a.m. Coast still on our port side. The wind is now getting colder and a little rain is falling.

Thursday, January 8th   Arrived Gibraltar 9.0 a.m. − towed into dock. Moored at Gun Wharf close to King's Stairs − taking coal aboard.

This rock is very high with cable lifts up to top. Big guns right on the top. Some fine buildings and big docks.

Took some ordnance stores and mail on and left the harbour at 8.0 p.m. Warm evening. Gibraltar looks a treat lighted up.

The guns on the Rock were 9.2 inch breach-loaded with a range of 20.9 miles. At this time there were 14 guns in 12 batteries. They took part in Gibraltar's only general action in the First World War on December 31st, 1915. German submarines were sighted, 13 rounds were fired with the result one target disappeared and a large explosion took place on another. One of these guns is on display at the Imperial War Museum, Duxford Airfield, Cambridgeshire.

Imperial War Museum

Friday, January 9th   Land on starboard side. Sea very calm.

Saturday, January 10th   Land on starboard side. Very heavy swell on − can't walk or stand. 2 p.m. − the boat is now tossing about in all directions. I expect we are near the Bay of Biscay.

Sunday, January 11th   We had a terrible night, being thrown about the boat like balls. Lost nearly all the dinner on the floor. At 1.30 we caught an extra wave which nearly turned us over and broke all the fittings in the cabins. All ordered below and everywhere battened down. At 5.15 p.m. a wave struck us and sent us spinning round, just like a collision. One man fell down the stairs and went in dock − about a dozen in there with broken ankles, arms, faces.

Monday, January 12th   Had another terrible night. Sighted the Lizard light at 10.0 p.m. then it was a bit quieter. Arrived behind Plymouth breakwater at 3.0 a.m., then cleaned up the rubbish.

Taken off by tender at 11 a.m. – landed at Great Western Railway docks. A military band was playing as we entered and remained giving us lively tunes until departure. We were given a meal to eat and another for the train. Placed seven men to a compartment.

Left Plymouth at 1.30 p.m., arrived at Purfleet at midnight.

Tuesday, January 13th   A tramp in the dark – we got to the camp at 12.30 a.m. Had a hot supper and slept in guard hut.

Paraded at 8.0 a.m. with all kit. Went through all the offices and was finished at 11.0 a.m. Marched to Purfleet station at 12.30 p.m. Train for London left at 12.45 p.m.

THE YEARS AFTER

Following his discharge on February 10th, 1920 Fred and Jessie continued to live in Ramsgate. In the 1920's he was involved in the alterations to Holy Trinity Church at Broadstairs which were carried out by the firm of John O. May, Builders of Broadstairs (*Jack* May was mentioned in the diaries). The same firm built "Seven Stones," a magnificent house on the cliff at Dumpton Gap. He was so proud of the craftsmenship which went into this house that successive generations of his family have been shown the photographs of the construction work. At some stage he was also involved in work at the Sandwich Town Hall.

Fred's Certificate of Transfer to Reserve.

What were they celebrating?
(Fred standing − third from the right)

Building in progress at "Seven Stones" − Fred wearing the white hat.

Roofing "Seven Stones".

"Seven Stones" was built to very high specifications in 1926–7 for a Mr. Paget, owner of The Crown Derby Potteries. The property has changed very little and no paint or wallpaper is ever used in its decoration. The house got its name from an experience the first owner had at sea when he was a young man. He was on one of his father's barges which was in danger of sinking; the captain told them to pray for their safety whereupon they came across The Seven Stones Lighthouse and were saved. Winston Churchill used the house for top-secret meetings during the last war.

Broadstairs Parish Church of the Holy Trinity (Church of England) was first built in 1829. Many improvements were made over the years; it was enlarged in 1914–15 and further work was carried out in 1924–25 when Uncle Fred was involved.

Sandwich Town Hall.

A proud Uncle Fred outside his own business premises.

All Fred's sisters married: Florence's two grandsons now live on Merseyside, but Jess's children died when young. Neither of Adela's two daughters had any children. Lily, eight years his senior, had three children who are all living in Kent with children and grandchildren of their own. Neither of his brothers had any surviving children.

Aunt Jessie

Uncle Fred

R 606

A sea-side stroll.

His mother, Caroline, died in September 1928 aged 87 and brother Will during the second World War in Ramsgate. Jessie died in 1939 at the age of 51, shortly after both her parents and Fred continued his father-in-law's business changing the name to Heffer-Mills. During the second World War he served in the Home Guard and was proud to have completed 21 years' voluntary army service. He had several serious eye operations, the first being at Moorfields Hospital in London.

In 1955 he retired from Greenhill Road, Harrow and moved to Boscombe in Hampshire. He continued to visit Kent regularly to attend regimental reunions.

Nine months before his death he moved to Broad Waters, a retirement home near Boscombe, and died in Poole General Hospital on 19th January 1978, just before his 95th birthday. He is survived by one nephew and two nieces, six great-nephews and nieces, and six great-great nephews and nieces.

Great Uncle Fred in the Home Guard.

Great Uncle Fred age 85.

Great Uncle Fred's Medals.   *Photo: Paul Dennis*

BRITISH WAR MEDAL
1914-1920 granted to all ranks of the services who rendered approved services overseas. All members of recognised or authorised organizations were eligible.

VICTORY MEDAL
Awarded to all ranks who took part in the Great War 1914 – 1918 and served in a theatre of war.

DEFENCE MEDAL
Awarded for three years service in the United Kingdom between 3rd September 1939 and 2nd September 1945 or for one year's service in an overseas non-operational theatre.

BUFFS Museum Canterbury

SOURCES OF INFORMATION

The Aeroplanes of The Royal Flying Corps. J. M. Bruce

A Brief Record of the Advance of the Egyptian Expeditionary Force, July 1917–October 1918.

British Military Aircraft Serials 1911–1979. Bruce Robertson. Patrick Stephens, 1979.

The Campaign in Palestine from the Enemy's Side. Col. Kress von Kressenstein. (Extract from *The Journal of the Royal United Services Institutions 1922).*

Encyclopaedia Britannica, Fourteenth edition, 1929–32.

Fighter Squadrons of the R.A.F. and Their Aircraft. John Rawlings. Macdonald and James, London, 1976.

Four Years Beneath the Crescent. Nogales. Charles Scribners 1926.

History of the Great War, Medical Services General History – Vol. 1 Maj. Gen. Sir W. G. Macpherson.

Imperial Camel Corps. Geoffrey Inchbald. Johnsons, London, 1970.

Jane's Fighting Ships 1919–1920

Lloyds' Register 1919

Military Wing. Putham & Co. Ltd.

Myself a Player. L. Ashwell. Michael Joseph Ltd., 1936.

My War Diary. S. Brown. John McQueen & Son, 1941.

Naval Notes 1914–1918. Naval Attache, British Embassy, Tokyo. Imperial War Museum Library.

The Official History of World War I

Tabers Cyclopedic Medical Dictionary. C. W. Tabor. F. A. Davis, 1952.

INDEX

C

Cablegrams: 16, 17
Cairo Water Company: 23
Category: 7, 8n
Casualties: 23n, 34n, 48n, 49n (see also Wounded)
Caucasus: XV
Censorship: 18
Christmas: 50, 51 (see also Food)
   Day: 27, 52, 73
   Presents: 25
Church Parades and Services: 13, 26, 50, 73
Civil Employment Form: 51
Clothing: 13, 24
   Drill clothes: 34, 60
   Goggles: 33
   Knickers: 22, 26
   Puttees: 42
   Sun helmet: 26, 34, 47, 60
Concert Party: 34, 38, 38n, 39, 46, 47 (see also Entertainments)
Construction work:
   Alterations to General Allenby's house: 57
   Blacksmiths: 33
   Bricklayers: 33, 34, 35
   Brickmaking: 34
   Brick wall for cemetery: 42
   Camp for tractor corps: 51
   Carpenters: 33
   Court Martial Room: 42
   Dam on the Sweet Water Canal: 24
   Flooring at H.Q.: 43
   Indian Base Depot: 33
   Paving lawn-tennis court: 45
   Pipe-laying: 32
   Pontoon Bridge: 66
   Prison cages and cells: 43, 45, 47
   Setting-out casings: 32
   Soda Water Factory: 68
   Water Filtering Plant: 23, 24n, 26
   Wheelwrights: 33
Contractors:
   Egyptian: 23
   Italian: 23

D

Demobilisation: 48, 54, 66, 68, 72, 73, 74, 75, 76, 77
Destroyers: (see also Ships)
   British: 14
   Japanese: 14, 18, 18n
Diaries:
   Captured diaries: 19n
   Fred's diaries: VII
   Regimental: 24n, 38n
Doctors: 39
Drink:
   Beer: 32, 50, 52
   Coffee: 17
   Rum: 58
   Tea: 10, 11, 12, 13, 14, 26, 28, 42
   Water: 11, 12, 39, 55

E

Egypt: III, XV
   Alexandria: 16, 35, 75
   Beersheba: XV, 22
   Cairo: 40, 41
   Gaza: XV, 22, 24, 68
   Giza: 40
   Ismailia: 16, 25, 49
   Kantara: 16, 24, 26, 29, 38, 42, 46, 47, 49, 53, 55, 57, 66, 68
   Nile: 40, 41
   Port Said: 32, 50
   Romani: 32
   Salt Water Lake: 25
   Sinai: XV
   Suez Canal: XV, 16, 17, 66
   Sweet Water Canal: 24, 39
   Tel El Kebir: 40, 41n
   Zagazig: 16, 33
Egyptians: 31, 39 (see also British and Colonial Troops: Egyptian Labour Corps)

L

Labourers: 33, 34, 37, 46 (see also British and Colonial Troops)
Lane, Stanley: 39
Language problems: 24, 33, 35
Lawrence: XV
Leave: 8, 9, 25, 38, 40, 41, 42, 53
Long, Will: 48

M

Mail: 13, 17, 18, 21, 22, 27, 50, 51, 52 (see also Censor)
Malta: 75
Matches: 12, 50
May, Jack: 42, 79
    John 0: 79
Medals: 87
    British War Medal: 87
    Defence: 87
    Victory: 87
Mediterranean: III, 55
Mesopotamia: XV, 31, 39, 52
    Baghdad: XV
Mills bomb: 32
Mills:
    Adela: 1, 83
    Alfred:1
    Caroline: 1, 84
    Florence: 1, 83
    Frederick: III, VII, 1, 2, 3, 4, 5, 7, 9, 30, 32, 52, 70, 71, 73, 79, 80, 83, 84, 85, 86, 87
    George: 1
    Jess: 1, 83
    Jessie: 4, 27, 51, 79, 83, 84
    Lily: 1, 83
    William: 2, 6, 9, 84
Mines: 14, 16
Money rates: 12, 14, 18, 65, 74
Mortar practice: 33

N

Newspapers: 21, 22, 62
Nurses: 11, 22, 27, 32, 42

O

Officers: 10, 33, 42, 46, 47
    Generals:
        Allenby: XV, 34n, 57
        Broadbent: 33
        Lloyd: 48, 49, 51
        Murray: XV
        Patin: 50
        Wright: 54
    Lieutenants:
        Lloyd-Williams: 62
        Steele, R. C.: 62
        Wibberley: 57

    Relations with men: 14, 15, 16, 17, 33, 42, 46, 47, 48, 50, 51, 53, 57
    Wibberley, Lieutenant: 57

Other ranks:
    Corporals: 15, 34, 48
        Clayson: 52
    Gunners:
        Eldridge: 53
    N.C.O.'s: 47, 57
    Sappers:
        Bagwell: 53
        Baker: 75
        Chandler: 42, 42n, 43
        Dunn: 53
        Gardner: 34, 35
        James: 65
        Kerswell: 46
        Till: 52
        Wallis, H.: 53
    Sergeants: 14, 42, 53, 65
        Simmonds: 46
Ottoman Empire: XV

T

Thorncroft: 38, 48
Tobacco: 10, 12, 21, 50
    Cigarettes: 10, 13
    Cigars: 28
Torpedo: 76n
    Torpedoed: 14
Troops: (see also British and Colonial Troops)
    Algerian: 11
    Australian: 17, 29
    Colonial: 35
    French: 10
    Indian: 33, 37, 65
    Italian: 11, 33
    Territorials: 18
    Turkish: 17
Turkey: XV
    Dardanelles: XV
    Gallipoli: XV
    Salonika: XV, 31
    Turks: XV

V

Vagabonds party: 46 (see also Entertainments)
Vehicles:
    Caterpillar Tractors: 51, 52
    Motor Lorries: 19n, 54n, 55n
    Tanks: 25n
    Trams: 12

W

Waters, P. C.: 54
Weather:
    Cold: 14, 24, 52
    Cyclonic storm: 24
    Hailstones: 32
    Heat: 11, 16, 25, 37, 42
    Lightning: 14, 34, 46
    Rain: 9, 12, 14, 24, 27, 32, 34, 45, 46, 56, 58, 72
    Sandstorm: 33, 34, 37, 38, 46, 72, 73
Western Front: III, 9, 34n
Wireless Station: 11
Women: 32, 33 (see also Nurses)
Wounded: 17, 21, 22, 23, 42, 48, 49n (see also Prisoners)

Y

Y.M.C.A.: 14, 55, 58, 65

Z

Zeppelin: 34

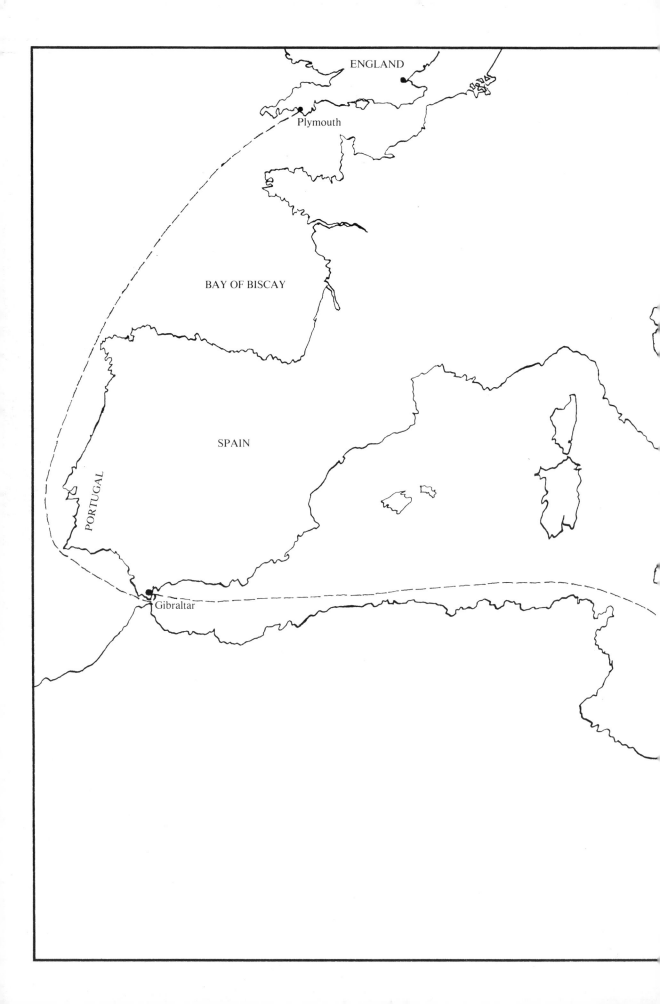